AF837087

Praise for *The Opportunity Zones Playbook*

"I am proud of what Opportunity Zones have achieved, but I am even more excited about what lies ahead. This book tells the story of how Opportunity Zones work and why they matter. At its core, it reflects a larger mission: expanding access to the American Dream."

US Senator Tim Scott (R-SC)
Chairman, Senate Committee on Banking, Housing, and Urban Affairs

"Opportunity Zones have taken private investment and breathed new life into cities and neighborhoods that haven't seen significant public sector investment in years. This book highlights those stories, and it shares how Opportunity Zones are revitalizing communities across the country, including in my home district in Erie, Pennsylvania."

US Representative Mike Kelly (PA-16)
Chairman, Ways & Means Subcommittee on Tax

"*The Opportunity Zones Playbook* provides investors, fund managers, and OZ fund advisors with a comprehensive, practical, and actionable guide on how to form, operate, profit, and exit from a variety of OZ investments. Jimmy has been a national OZ influencer since the OZ program's passage in 2017, and this book encapsulates his deep knowledge on this powerful and flexible economic development program."

Blake Christian, CPA
Partner, HCVT

"Few people have engaged as deeply with as many Opportunity Zone stakeholders as Jimmy Atkinson, and that breadth of perspective is evident throughout this exceptionally comprehensive and practical guide to a subject that is often misunderstood. He has done a real service by publishing this book at exactly the right moment, when a clear and practical playbook is needed for the next generation of those living, working, and investing in the American communities that need it most."

Andrew P. Doup
Managing Attorney, SyndicationCounsel LLC

"Jimmy has been a foundational force in the OZ community since its inception, helping to bridge the gap between private capital and community impact. *The Opportunity Zones Playbook* is a masterclass in the evolution of the program, proving once again why Jimmy remains the most trusted voice in the industry."

Michael Episcope
Co-CEO, Origin Investments

"*The Opportunity Zones Playbook* is the most practical and insightful guide I've seen for navigating and capitalizing on Opportunity Zone investing. After working with Jimmy Atkinson for over seven years—appearing on his podcasts, presenting alongside him, and partnering through his pitch events—I can personally attest that his expertise has helped Urban Catalyst raise millions of dollars for our Opportunity Zone funds and deliver real results for investors."

Erik Hayden
Founder and Managing Partner, Urban Catalyst

"Since the early days of Opportunity Zones, Jimmy Atkinson has played a unique role in bringing together investors, fund managers, and policymakers while building a trusted source of education for the OZ community. *The Opportunity Zones Playbook* captures those years of insight and conversation, providing a practical guide for those looking to understand and participate in the Opportunity Zones market."

Jill Homan
Deputy Director of Economy & Trade, America First Policy Institute

"*The Opportunity Zones Playbook* is an essential resource for anyone seeking to understand, structure, and invest in Opportunity Zones with confidence and clarity. Jimmy Atkinson brings together deep policy expertise and real-world experience to deliver a practical, actionable guide for investors, fund managers, and community leaders alike."

Emily Lavery
Senior Vice President, Fulcrum Public Affairs

"Most people hear about Opportunity Zones after a major liquidity event, a business sale, a real estate exit, a stock windfall, and have no idea where to begin. This book is where you begin. Jimmy has spent years making OZs accessible to real investors, and this playbook is the best version of that work. Clear, thorough, and built for action."

Barrett Linburg
Co-Founder & CEO, Savoy

"Jimmy has been a dedicated industry leader, providing a range of comprehensive and accessible resources on the Opportunity Zones policy and how to put it to use. This book is the product of years of research and conversations with leaders and practitioners across the country. It should serve as a seminal guide for anyone looking to invest in OZs, advise their clients, or sponsor an OZ project."

Catherine Lyons
Director of Policy, Economic Innovation Group

"Jimmy's work in the Opportunity Zone space is second to none. He was there day one and has been an active, engaged, can-do gatherer of investors, developers, owners and funds ever since. His education sessions and OZ Pitch Days are nationally well known, well regarded and attended by thousands. *The Opportunity Zones Playbook* is the next iteration of his sharing of knowledge and represents one of the definitive resources for those looking to better understand and invest in Opportunity Zones. I highly recommend to all my OZ clients that the *Playbook* be on their respective bookshelves for an easy to navigate definitive reference."

Brad A. Molotsky
Partner, FisherBroyles

"Jimmy has worked tirelessly since 2018 to become the GOAT for QOZs. The substance in this book solidifies that title! Jimmy is the go-to platform for all things QOZ. Of course, there are attorneys, CPAs, developers, sponsors, investors and others all with substantial knowledge, but Jimmy has developed the platform that consolidates it all. Jimmy's book is yet another excellent substantive resource for anyone at any level of knowledge. It is easy to read and is an excellent how-to for the Qualified Opportunity Zone Program."

Coni Rathbone
Of Counsel, VF Law

"I've known and collaborated with Jimmy Atkinson since the earliest days of the Opportunity Zone initiative, when we both recognized its extraordinary potential as a new investment and tax incentive framework. Driven by an entrepreneurial energy I deeply admire, Jimmy has built platforms, communities and resources that have become essential for professionals across the Opportunity Zone ecosystem. Over the years he has earned a reputation as one of the most trusted voices in the industry, helping investors, developers, fund sponsors, and advisors better understand and make use of both the promise and the practical realities of Opportunity Zone investing. This book distills that experience into a clear, thoughtful guide that will be valuable to both newcomers and seasoned practitioners alike."

Gerald J. Reihsen, III
Corporate Securities Attorney, Reihsen & Associates

"Jimmy Atkinson is the Jedi master of the Opportunity Zone universe."

Louis Rogers
Founder and Co-CEO, Capital Square
Author of *Section 1031 Exchanges: How to Swap Till Ya' Drop, Building Family Wealth While Minimizing Taxes*

"Opportunity Zones are one of the most powerful incentives in the tax code, but they require careful planning to use correctly. Jimmy Atkinson understands both the policy and the psychology behind Opportunity Zones, and in *The Opportunity Zones Playbook* he does an excellent job breaking down the strategy, structure, and real-world mechanics into a clear, practical roadmap for investors and advisors looking to make OZs a meaningful part of their long-term tax and investment strategy."

Mr. Ashley Tison
Founder and President, OZPros

"Opportunity Zones 1.0 proved we could mobilize disconnected capital; OZ 2.0 demands we know how to deploy it for maximum economic intensity. Now that OZs are a permanent fixture of our tax code, there's an enormous opportunity to use this creative structure to help transform our nation's communities. Jimmy Atkinson's *The Opportunity Zones Playbook* isn't just a review of past policy; it is the essential blueprint for anyone looking to understand the promise that Opportunity Zones present for the next decade of investing and community stabilization."

Jonathan Tower
Founder & CEO, Arctaris Impact Investors

"*The Opportunity Zones Playbook* provides a thoughtful and well-researched history of the OZ incentive, placing its origins, policy objectives, and evolution into clear context. It has earned a prominent place on my bookshelf as a go-to educational resource for practitioners, investors, and policymakers seeking a deeper understanding of the OZ incentive."

Jason Watkins, CPA
Partner, Novogradac & Company
Chairman, Novogradac Opportunity Zones Working Group

THE OPPORTUNITY ZONES PLAYBOOK

Master the OZ Tax Incentive to Build Wealth, Fund Deals, and Create Impact

BY JIMMY ATKINSON

Kingsbury Media
FORT WORTH, TEXAS

The Opportunity Zones Playbook
Master the OZ Tax Incentive to Build Wealth, Fund Deals, and Create Impact

Published by Kingsbury Media
Fort Worth, Texas

A Note to Readers

This book shares information and perspectives on Opportunity Zone investing but is not a substitute for professional advice. Tax laws and regulations evolve, and readers should confirm the latest rules with qualified advisors. Nothing in these pages should be construed as legal, tax, or investment advice. Please consult your attorney, CPA, or financial advisor before making any investment decisions.

Names: Atkinson, Jimmy, author.
Title: The opportunity zones playbook : master the oz tax incentive to build wealth, fund deals, and create impact / by Jimmy Atkinson.
Description: Fort Worth, Texas : Kingsbury Media, [2026] | Includes bibliographical references and index.
Identifiers: LCCN: 2026906233 | ISBN: 9798995038924 (hardcover) | ISBN: 9798995038900 (paperback) | 9798995038917 (ebook) Subjects: LCSH: Investments. | Deferred tax—United States. | Investment tax credit—United States. | Capital gains tax—United States. | Real estate development—United States. | Community development—Taxation—United States. | Economic development—Taxation—United States. | Enterprise zones—Taxation—United States. | Real estate investment trusts—Taxation—United States. | Mutual funds—United States. | Wealth. | Finance, Personal. | BISAC: BUSINESS & ECONOMICS / Investments & Securities / Real Estate. | BUSINESS & ECONOMICS / Personal Finance / Investing. | BUSINESS & ECONOMICS / Personal Finance / Taxation. | BUSINESS & ECONOMICS / Development / Economic Development.
Classification: LCC: HG4521 .A85 2026 | DDC: 332.6—dc23

For information, contact:
info@opportunityzones.com
https://opportunityzones.com

Hardcover ISBN: 979-8-9950389-2-4
Paperback ISBN: 979-8-9950389-0-0
E-book ISBN: 979-8-9950389-1-7

Edited by Andy Hagans

For my wife, Natalie, and my children, Julia, James, and Kate.

CONTENTS

FOREWORD BY

Senator Tim Scott

I grew up in North Charleston, South Carolina, raised by a single mother who worked long hours to keep food on the table and a roof over our heads. She left early each morning and returned late at night, determined that her sons would have a better future than the circumstances into which we were born.

Our neighborhood was filled with talent and resilience. What it lacked was capital.

Storefronts sat empty. Investment skipped over entire blocks. Hardworking families did everything right and still found themselves waiting for opportunity to arrive. I learned early that the difference between struggle and stability was often not effort, but access. Access to jobs. Access to financing. Access to someone willing to invest in a community others had written off.

Those experiences shaped my belief that while government cannot transform communities on its own, it can help create the conditions for capital to flow where it has not flowed before.

Opportunity Zones were born from that conviction.

When Senator Cory Booker and I first introduced Opportunity Zones legislation in 2016, we set out to turn that belief into policy. We wanted to unlock private capital and direct it into communities that had been overlooked for decades.

The idea was simple: reward long-term investment in low-income areas instead of concentrating capital in neighborhoods already thriving.

Before Opportunity Zones, too many communities were labeled "too risky." Private investment flowed into markets that were already strong, while distressed neighborhoods struggled to attract capital.

After President Trump signed Opportunity Zones into law in 2017, we began to see a shift.

Cranes returned to long-dormant skylines. Housing was built. Entrepreneurs found financing. Jobs followed investment. Billions of dollars in private capital moved into communities that had not seen sustained investment in a generation.

Policies of this magnitude require refinement. Over time, we improved transparency, strengthened reporting, and ensured the incentive continued to serve its purpose. Most importantly, we provided certainty. Economic revitalization does not operate on election cycles. It requires stability and a long-term horizon.

That is why making Opportunity Zones permanent was so critical.

By securing permanence in the One Big Beautiful Bill Act in 2025, we sent a clear signal: the Opportunity Zones policy is not an experiment. It is a lasting tool for economic empowerment. Investors can plan for the long term. Communities can build with confidence. Families can trust that opportunity is not temporary.

I am proud of what Opportunity Zones have achieved, but I am even more excited about what lies ahead. When government creates the right framework and steps back, the private sector can do extraordinary things.

This book tells the story of how Opportunity Zones work and why they matter. At its core, it reflects a larger mission: expanding access to the American Dream.

America will never be a country where a zip code determines your destiny. Opportunity Zones represent a commitment to that promise.

For me, the Opportunity Zones policy has always been personal. It is rooted in my own journey and in the belief that talent is universal, even when opportunity is not. By mobilizing capital and fostering partnership between the public and private sectors, we are proving that revitalization is possible.

The work continues. The impact is real. And the promise of stronger communities and brighter futures is only beginning to be fulfilled.

US Senator Tim Scott

PREFACE

An American Revival

Hidden across the American map lies a mysterious patchwork, thousands of overlooked pockets in our cities, suburbs, and rural communities. On the surface, these places may seem ordinary, even distressed and forgotten. Strip malls with vacant storefronts. Industrial corridors that haven't seen new construction in decades. Small towns left behind by globalization. But beneath the surface, a transformation is quietly unfolding, one fueled by capital, tax code, and a rare alignment of public policy and private ambition.

These areas are known as Opportunity Zones.

Created in 2017 through the Tax Cuts and Jobs Act, the Opportunity Zones program began as a bipartisan experiment in economic development. It gave investors a powerful incentive: redirect your capital gains into long-term investments in designated economically distressed areas, and in return, you could defer, reduce, and eliminate your tax liabilities.

It is, in this author's view, the most powerful tax-advantaged investment opportunity in modern US history.

Since then, billions of dollars have flowed in. Real estate deals have been inked. Businesses have been launched, and ground has been broken. At their best, Opportunity Zones have become vehicles for revitalization, turning forgotten lots into housing, capital deserts into job engines, and underinvested communities into growth markets. A new kind of investor has emerged—one willing to trade liquidity for patience, and short-term gains for a decade of compounding.

Now we are entering the next era.

With the passage of the One Big Beautiful Bill Act in 2025,

Opportunity Zones have been reborn. The program is now permanent. The eligibility map has been redrawn, rural communities have received new attention and incentive, and the deferral timeline has been simplified for investors. OZ 2.0 is not a patch on the original; it's a reimagining of it. A new game, with higher stakes and sharper strategy.

The map is changing. The rules are evolving. And the opportunity may be bigger than ever.

If you are holding this book, chances are you have capital at stake. Maybe you've recently realized a gain. Maybe you're a developer staring at a site in a Qualified Opportunity Zone and wondering how the program can help with your capital raise. Maybe you're an advisor trying to make sense of evolving guidance, compliance obligations, and the promise of OZ 2.0. Or maybe you're simply trying to determine whether Opportunity Zones are the real thing or just another tax fad.

I wrote this book for you.

Opportunity Zones are both simpler and more complex than most people think. The core incentive is straightforward: reinvest capital gains, defer taxes, and, if you stay long enough, eliminate taxes on new appreciation. But the execution is anything but simple.

In the years since this program was enacted, I've interviewed fund managers, developers, attorneys, accountants, policymakers, and investors. I've watched capital flow into multifamily projects, industrial developments, self-storage facilities, defense manufacturing, historic rehabs, and startup businesses. I've also seen projects stall, funds struggle, and sponsors miscalculate.

Opportunity Zones are not magic. They are a tool.

Used thoughtfully, they can unlock patient capital, align incentives, and catalyze durable economic growth. Used carelessly, they can amplify risk, obscure underwriting weaknesses, and distract from fundamentals.

And yes, I believe in the Opportunity Zones program.

I believe it represents one of the most powerful economic development policies of our lifetime. I believe it can drive meaningful private investment into communities that have been capital-starved for generations. And I believe it rewards long-term thinking in a financial system too often dominated by short-term incentives.

So if this book feels like an argument for Opportunity Zones, that's because it is.

But it is not an argument for blind optimism. It is an argument for disciplined execution. For thoughtful structuring. For responsible capital allocation. For understanding both the upsides and the risks. For treating this incentive not as a loophole, but as a long-term partnership between investors and communities.

This book is your compass, your decoder ring, and your tactical playbook. Whether you're a high-net-worth investor looking to defer and grow your gains, a developer or fund sponsor seeking capital, or an advisor helping clients navigate the program, *The Opportunity Zones Playbook* will guide you through the legal, strategic, and practical frameworks that matter most.

In the land of Opportunity Zones, timing matters. Structure matters. And, most of all, knowing where to look and when to act matters.

Let's begin.

Jimmy Atkinson

THE OPPORTUNITY ZONES PLAYBOOK

INTRODUCTION

The Greatest Tax Incentive Ever Invented

It's funny how life-changing moments often arrive quietly.

There was no big announcement, no lightning bolt. It was just a headline on a podcast app. On the evening of August 1, 2018, I was sitting on my couch, casually scrolling through my phone, when a podcast title caught my attention: "You Don't Pay Any New Capital Gains—Ever."[1]

Naturally, that stopped me cold.

I hit play.

What then followed was an hour-long introduction to something I had never heard of before: Opportunity Zones.

The episode featured Steve Glickman from the Economic Innovation Group, one of the architects of the OZ policy, and by the time the episode ended, something had shifted. This wasn't just a clever tax strategy. Nor was it some gimmicky loophole. It was something different, a *bipartisan* incentive designed to redirect capital into America's most overlooked communities, while offering extraordinary tax advantages to those who invested.

It felt rare, like a secret hiding in plain sight, the kind of opportunity you stumble into once *if* you're lucky enough to recognize it. That night, I couldn't stop thinking about it. I stayed up late digging

---

1. Steve Glickman, guest, *The Meb Faber Show*, "Episode #115: Ultimately, If You Hold for. . . 10 Years or More. . . You Don't Pay Any New Capital Gains–Ever," Meb Faber Research, August 1, 2018, https://mebfaber.com/2018/08/01/episode-115-steve-glickman-opportunity-zones-ultimately-if-you-hold-for10-years-or-moreyou-dont-pay-any-new-capital-gains-ever/

through articles, policy papers—whatever I could find. But there wasn't much. The few resources that existed were mostly written for tax attorneys and accountants.

There was nothing that explained the program clearly to investors, developers, or the public at large.

That's when I saw the opportunity. Before the clock struck midnight, I had purchased the domain name OpportunityDb.com. I had no grand plan, just a feeling that this program could be huge and that someone needed to explain it.

So I started building.

The Platform that Launched a Movement

Over the next few months, what began as a late-night curiosity turned into a full-time mission.

I poured myself into building the site, day after day, often late into the night from my home office. The early version was scrappy, simple, and a bit rough around the edges, but it had a clear purpose: to connect investors with Opportunity Zone funds and projects and to help them understand how the incentive really worked.

At the time, there was no playbook, no proven model. I didn't know if anyone would visit the site, let alone use it. But I had a hunch: if even a small percentage of investors understood the scale of the tax benefits available, this program could take off.

By the end of 2018, I was posting content regularly, sharing updates, breaking down technical articles from attorneys and accountants, and trying to make Opportunity Zones accessible for real people. Slowly but surely, a small audience began to form.

Then, in January 2019, everything changed.

I flew to Los Angeles to attend the first-ever Opportunity Zone Expo at the JW Marriott. I had no booth, no speaking slot, and barely any connections. I was just an attendee, still figuring it all out, unsure what to expect, or even what to wear.

As I stepped into that ballroom, I felt it instantly: the energy was real. There were hundreds of people, buzzing with questions and optimism. The event organizers had underestimated the turnout. I remember standing in the crowd, watching the room fill up, and thinking to myself: *This thing is way bigger than I realized.*

The Inflection Point

That day in Los Angeles was more than just a good event. It was an inflection point—for me, and for the entire OZ industry.

Up until then, I had been building in a vacuum: publishing content, testing ideas, working in the dark. In that packed ballroom, surrounded by hundreds of people from across the country—fund managers, developers, attorneys, accountants, advisors, and curious investors—I realized something crucial: *This wasn't a niche. This was a movement.*

From that moment forward, I doubled down.

OpportunityDb (later rebranded to OpportunityZones.com) began to grow by leaps and bounds. I launched *The Opportunity Zones Podcast*. I created the first national online OZ investor showcase event, called OZ Pitch Day, which would go on to connect tens of millions of dollars in capital with dozens of Opportunity Zone projects. I started an email newsletter that would eventually reach more than 20,000 subscribers. I formed a private mastermind community, OZ Insiders, for high intent developers, investors, and professionals.

Podcast by podcast, webinar by webinar, event by event, my momentum compounded, as I steadily helped to shape this industry one conversation at a time. Two big things changed for me after that January 2019 event.

First, I went from being a nervous attendee soaking up information to a recognized authority. Today, I'm often invited to speak at the very conferences I once walked into wide-eyed and uncertain.

Second, I started forming real relationships with policymakers in Washington, as well as real estate developers, fund sponsors, attorneys, accountants, and fellow entrepreneurs. We were all trying to figure this thing out, together.

A Cloud Over the Industry

Even as the Opportunity Zones industry grew, and my own platform along with it, there was always one big caveat looming in the background: the clock was ticking.

The OZ program, as originally designed, was temporary. Gains generated after December 31, 2026, would no longer be eligible for Opportunity Zone investment. That expiration date cast a long shadow over the program. It spooked wealth advisors. It paralyzed cautious investors. It made developers second-guess OZ strategies—even in markets where they made perfect sense.

To me, it always felt like the biggest thing holding the industry back. Not the complexity of the rules. Not the learning curve. Not even the market dynamics. Just the uncertainty of whether the program would stick around.

Behind the scenes, though, momentum was building. There were congresspeople on both sides of the aisle who believed in the program, who had seen the data, who had heard from their constituents.[2] And who knew this wasn't just a tax break but also a long-term engine for local investment, entrepreneurship, and job creation.

The only question was timing.

A Second Beginning

That question was answered decisively on July 4, 2025, the day President Donald Trump signed the One Big Beautiful Bill Act into law.[3] Tucked inside the hundreds of pages of legislation was a section that would change everything for the Opportunity Zones industry. The sunset date was gone, the program was made permanent, and a new chapter had officially begun.[4]

---

2. "History of Opportunity Zones," Economic Innovation Group, accessed October 30, 2025, https://eig.org/opportunity-zones/about-ozs.

3. One Big Beautiful Bill Act, Pub. L. No. 119-21, 139 Stat. 72 (2025).

4. "Senate Passes Opportunity Zones 2.0 Legislation," OpportunityZones.com, July 1, 2025, https://opportunityzones.com/2025/07/senate-bill-passes-350/

The OZ program wasn't just extended. It was *upgraded*—reshaped, refined, and reaffirmed as a permanent feature of the US tax code. Among the enhancements:

- a new map of Opportunity Zones, set to take effect in 2027;[5]
- a rolling five-year deferral period for new investors;
- special tax incentives for rural investments; and
- expanded reporting requirements to ensure transparency and accountability.

This was Opportunity Zones 2.0, and it sent a clear message: the program was no longer a policy experiment. It was here to stay.

For the financial industry, the writing was on the wall. OZs were no longer fringe; they were mainstream. Financial advisors could no longer ignore them, and developers as well as fund managers had new tools to work with. Investors now had the green light to make long-term commitments with confidence.

For me personally, it was the moment I had been preparing for since 2018. The moment that validated all the years of content, events, education, and relationship-building. The OZ industry had matured, and now, the runway had been extended.

The Greatest Tax Incentive Ever Created

Since I first learned about Opportunity Zones, I've often called them "the greatest tax incentive ever created." And I stand by that. Why? Because OZs aren't just flexible. They're transformative, especially for those who know how to use them.

Unlike other federal economic development tools, OZs don't require permission. There's no gatekeeper. No federal application. No approval process. No bureaucratic red tape. If you have a capital gain and a qualified investment, you can participate. Period. But what

---

5. The new map will take effect on January 1, 2027. But the map will be known weeks ahead of this effective date, likely in fall 2026. Check the OZ map on my website for the latest updates: https://opportunityzones.com/map/

truly sets Opportunity Zones apart is the tax treatment: powerful, elegant, and completely unmatched.

Here are the tax incentives available to OZ investors:

- deferral of eligible capital gains[6] (and the associated tax bill) until a future date;
- reduction of the gain that ultimately gets recognized (which may reduce the taxes owed);
- elimination of all tax on the appreciation of your new OZ investment—if held for at least ten years; and
- no depreciation recapture, a rare and significant advantage over traditional real estate investments that enhances after-tax returns.

Let me be very clear: the ability to eliminate capital gains tax within your lifetime (not just defer it, not just pass it on to your heirs, but eliminate it) is extraordinary.

Even the beloved 1031 exchange can't compete. With a 1031, you're deferring, but not escaping, capital gains. The tax eventually comes due, unless you die first.[7] With OZs, that escape hatch exists while you're still alive (after a ten-year hold).

Compared to a Roth IRA, OZs offer more flexibility. Roths are funded with after-tax dollars, have income restrictions, and cap how much you can contribute. In contrast, OZs have no income limits and no cap on the amount of gain you can roll into a Qualified Opportunity Fund (QOF).

Let's not forget: this isn't some obscure loophole buried in the footnotes. The OZ program is codified in Section 1400Z of the Internal Revenue Code.[8] It was created in 2017 through the Tax Cuts and Jobs Act and strengthened in 2025 through the One Big Beautiful Bill Act.

---

6. For the purposes of this book, I use the terms "gains" or "capital gains" to refer to eligible gains, which include capital gains and qualified Section 1231 gains (typically taxed at capital gains rates). Both short-term and long-term gains can qualify under the Opportunity Zones program.

7. "Opportunity Zones vs. 1031 Exchanges," OpportunityZones.com, updated December 31, 2025, https://opportunityzones.com/guide/oz-vs-1031/

8. Tax Cuts and Jobs Act, Pub. L. No. 115-97, 131 Stat. 2054 (2017).

It's real. It's intentional. It's bipartisan. And it might just be the most powerful wealth-building tool of our generation, while also directing billions into communities that need it most.

Why I Wrote This Book

Since I first listened to that podcast in 2018, Opportunity Zones have shaped the direction of my career and, frankly, my identity. I'm an investor, an entrepreneur, a content creator, and an educator. Previously, I had built websites from my high school bedroom and my college dorm room. But OpportunityZones.com was different. It wasn't just a project. It became a *mission*.

From day one, my goal has been simple: To make OZs accessible and understandable for the people who actually use them. Not just the tax attorneys and policy wonks. Real people like:

- investors with big capital gains;
- developers with ambitious projects;
- advisors trying to help clients navigate the code; and
- economic leaders trying to attract investment to their communities.

Along the way, I launched the podcast, the email newsletter, the OZ Pitch Day event series, and the OZ Insiders mastermind community.

And yet, even with all of that going on, I kept noticing the same thing: there was still a massive knowledge gap among high-net-worth investors, financial advisors, CPAs, real estate professionals, and even fund managers. I wrote this book to close that gap once and for all.

What This Book Will Teach You

This isn't just a book about tax law. It's a strategic playbook.

This book is for anyone looking to use Opportunity Zones as a tool for long-term, tax-smart investing. Whether you're sitting on a major capital gain or raising capital for a qualified deal, this book gives you the framework you need to navigate OZ 2.0 with clarity and confidence.

To keep things simple and actionable, this book is broken down into three parts:

PART I: FOUNDATIONS

I begin with the basics: what Opportunity Zones are, how they work, and what changed under OZ 2.0. This section will cover:

- the legislative history and purpose behind the program;
- the anatomy of the OZ tax benefits: deferral, reduction, and elimination; and
- key compliance and timing rules you *must* understand to stay eligible.

This section is your onboarding, whether you're brand new to OZs or need a refresher before diving deeper.

PART II: THE INVESTOR PLAYBOOK

This section is designed for:

- high-net-worth individuals;
- family offices;
- financial advisors; and
- anyone sitting on capital gains who wants to invest wisely.

You'll learn:

- a five-step framework for evaluating and timing your OZ investments;
- the difference between single-asset and multi-asset OZ funds;
- how to vet deals and sponsors effectively; and
- how to plan for the ten-year hold and exit.

If you have gains—from a business sale, stock portfolio, crypto, or real estate—this section will show you how to reposition that wealth for maximum after-tax return.

PART III: THE FUND AND DEAL SPONSOR PLAYBOOK

If you're on the other side of the table—maybe you're a developer, entrepreneur, or fund manager—this section is for you.

You'll learn:

- how to launch and structure your own Qualified Opportunity Fund;
- the difference between captive and professionally managed funds;
- how to operate a Qualified Opportunity Zone Business (QOZB);
- what it takes to raise capital in this ecosystem; and
- how to exit cleanly after more than ten years and deliver maximum value to investors.

This section distills years of experience from our community, events, and interviews into a battle-tested strategy guide for OZ operators.

WHO THIS BOOK IS FOR AND WHY IT MATTERS NOW

Opportunity Zones aren't for everyone. They're for people with something to gain and something to build.

This book is written for:

- high-net-worth investors looking to shelter capital gains and compound tax-free growth;
- family offices managing multi-generational wealth;
- real estate developers structuring new projects in growth markets;
- fund sponsors and entrepreneurs raising capital through OZs;
- CPAs, attorneys, and financial advisors helping clients navigate complex investments; and
- economic development leaders who want to attract OZ capital to their communities.

If that's you (or your clients), this book will show you how to use the Opportunity Zones program intelligently, strategically, and effectively. And there's no better time than now. In 2027, OZ 2.0 debuts with a brand-new map, a fresh ten-year runway, and a redesigned incentive that's stronger than ever.

The groundwork has already been laid. The dollars are already out there. The new zones are being drawn. And the window to act—to get ahead of this next wave—is open now.

Let's build.

PART I

FOUNDATIONS

CHAPTER ONE

WHAT ARE OPPORTUNITY ZONES?

OPPORTUNITY ZONES WERE CREATED to unlock long-term capital for underserved, disinvested communities across the United States. Their origin story began in the wake of the Great Recession of 2007–2009, a seismic event that widened the fault lines of American inequality. While affluent zip codes and metro areas rebounded swiftly, lower-income communities were left behind, their recoveries slow or nonexistent.[9] In fact, many remained in decline, disconnected from capital markets and forgotten by the broader economic expansion.[10]

This lopsided recovery posed a fundamental question: Could public policy help reverse the trend by redirecting private capital into the places that needed it most?

That answer began to take shape in 2015, when the Economic Innovation Group (EIG), a bipartisan think tank in Washington, DC,

---

9. "The Great Recession and Its Aftermath," Federal Reserve History, November 22, 2013, https://www.federalreservehistory.org/essays/great-recession-and-its-aftermath

10. There are numerous studies on this. An article from Axios cites EIG research that points to geographic unevenness of the recovery: https://www.axios.com/2018/05/24/economic-growth-disparities-recovery-great-recession. A report by the Pew Research Center studies the unevenness by household net worth: https://www.pewresearch.org/social-trends/2013/04/23/a-rise-in-wealth-for-the-wealthydeclines-for-the-lower-93/

published a white paper with a provocative title: "Unlocking Private Capital to Facilitate Economic Growth in Distressed Areas."[11] It would become the intellectual blueprint for the Opportunity Zones policy. It wasn't just another wonky policy report, though. It was a pioneering proposal, and what set it apart was the coalition behind it.

The authors were from opposite ends of the political spectrum: Kevin Hassett, a Republican economist affiliated with the American Enterprise Institute, and Jared Bernstein, a Democrat from the Center on Budget and Policy Priorities. Bernstein had served as an economic advisor in the Obama administration (and would later join President Joe Biden's team). Hassett would go on to advise President Donald Trump.

That unlikely collaboration laid the groundwork for what Opportunity Zones would ultimately become: a rare, bipartisan alliance forged around a common goal—to give disinvested communities a shot at long-term, market-based revitalization.

The concept took its first real step toward law in April 2016, when Senators Tim Scott (R-SC) and Cory Booker (D-NJ) introduced the Investing in Opportunity Act.[12] This bill proposed a revolutionary idea: to use tax incentives to encourage investment in designated low-income areas. Backed by a broad coalition in both the House and Senate, the policy had political momentum.

"When I first introduced Opportunity Zones legislation in 2016, we were focused on one central challenge: too many distressed communities were rich in potential but starved of long-term investment capital," says Senator Scott. "For decades, capital had flowed around these neighborhoods instead of into them, limiting job creation and economic mobility. We believed a market-driven incentive could unlock private investment, empower local leadership, and help transform over-

---

11. Jared Bernstein and Kevin A. Hassett, "Unlocking Private Capital to Facilitate Economic Growth in Distressed Areas," Economic Innovation Group, April 2015, https://eig.org/wp-content/uploads/2015/04/Unlocking-Private-Capital-to-Facilitate-Growth.pdf

12. Investing in Opportunity Act, S. 2868, 114th Cong. (2016).

looked communities from the inside out. At its heart, Opportunity Zones were about restoring hope by expanding access to opportunity."[13]

The following year, a new version of the bill attracted even more support: fourteen Senate co-sponsors (seven Republicans and seven Democrats),[14] and eighty-one House co-sponsors (forty-five Republicans and thirty-six Democrats).[15] Still, the bill didn't pass on its own.

But in late 2017, the tide turned. The OZ concept was folded into the sweeping Tax Cuts and Jobs Act, the signature tax legislation of President Trump's first term. When the TCJA was signed into law on December 22, 2017, the Opportunity Zones program was born.

What followed was nothing short of historic: a federal experiment in economic revitalization, built not on government spending but on a new kind of partnership—one where tax incentives would steer private investment into communities long overlooked. In just the first six years, the program helped mobilize more than $150 billion in private equity investments into communities that had long been overlooked.[16]

And it is a program that enjoys broad bipartisan support. According to US Representative Mike Kelly (R-PA), Chairman of the Ways and Means Subcommittee on Tax, revitalizing cities appeals to both ends of the political spectrum.

"To me, investing in our cities is neither a red issue nor a blue issue," says Kelly. "It's a red, white, and blue issue. I think Opportunity Zones have delivered exactly that—an opportunity to grow and revitalize neighborhoods that haven't seen significant private investment in decades."[17]

---

13. Tim Scott (US Senator), via email with the author, March 3, 2026.

14. Investing in Opportunity Act, S. 293, 115th Cong. (2017).

15. Investing in Opportunity Act, H.R. 828, 115th Cong. (2017).

16. This is an estimate of the amount of equity raised by Qualified Opportunity Funds through year-end 2023. Because most commercial real estate projects are typically funded with less than 50 percent equity, it's reasonable to assume that well in excess of $300 billion of private capital has flowed into Opportunity Zones.

17. Mike Kelly (US Representative), via email with the author, January 8, 2026.

The Opportunity Zones initiative wasn't just another tax break. It was a new playbook for economic development, one that defied traditional assumptions. It signaled to investors, developers, and entrepreneurs that there was now a tax-advantaged path to making a difference, all while pursuing competitive returns.

The Geography of Distress

The OZ program is, by definition, a *place-based* economic development policy. That means the tax incentives only apply to investments made in specific, geographically defined areas, namely, census tracts certified by the United States Department of the Treasury as Qualified Opportunity Zones.

Geography matters because, in America, your zip code often shapes your destiny.[18] Economic mobility is shaped by geography, and many distressed neighborhoods struggle to attract capital, not because they lack potential, but because traditional investment flows actively avoid them. Investors chase yield, and these places don't always scream opportunity.

That's the problem.

This isn't a theory. Decades of research have revealed a stubborn truth: where you grow up shapes how far you can go; it influences everything from income and education to health, mobility, and life expectancy.[19]

From a policy perspective, the insight is profound: if we want to change outcomes, we may need to change the flow of capital itself.

That's what Opportunity Zones do. Instead of top-down subsidies or endless grants, the policy flips the federal script: it invites

---

18. Raj Chetty et al., "The Fading American Dream: Trends in Absolute Income Mobility Since 1940," *Science* 356, no. 6336 (2017): 398–406, https://www.science.org/doi/10.1126/science.aal4617

19. Patrick Edwards, "The Impact of Neighborhood Disparities on Intergenerational Mobility and Economic Growth in the United States," Washington Center for Equitable Growth, December 1, 2021, https://equitablegrowth.org/the-impact-of-neighborhood-disparities-on-intergenerational-mobility-and-economic-growth-in-the-united-states/

private investors to participate not through mandates or handouts, but through incentives. And it comes with a simple offer: put long-term capital into a distressed neighborhood, and the tax code will reward you.

But there's a catch—and it's by design. OZ investments aren't meant for quick flips or short-term arbitrage. To unlock the full benefit, the capital must stay planted for at least ten years. In that time, the neighborhood has the chance to evolve alongside the investment. This structure sends a deeper message: *where* we invest matters. Capital isn't neutral; it has geography, values, and consequences. With the right incentives and a long enough timeline, we can align private interests with the public good. That's the genius of OZs.

In that sense, Opportunity Zones are more than a tax incentive; they are a moral investment strategy. They challenge investors to think not just about returns, but about place, permanence, and purpose. One community at a time.

Drawing the OZ Map: "Gerrymander" for Growth

When you think of bureaucrats drawing maps, you probably imagine gerrymandering: politicians twisting boundaries into bizarre shapes to protect their own power.

But when OZs were created, the mapmaking had a different purpose: channeling long-term private capital into distressed communities. This time, the lines weren't drawn to keep politicians safe, but to give communities a fighting chance.

The legislation didn't just sketch a vague idea. It laid out a detailed, statutory process for determining which areas would qualify.

The first key detail: Opportunity Zones had to be designated at the census tract level. These are relatively small, statistically defined areas used by the US Census Bureau to collect and analyze data.

Each tract typically includes between 1,200 and 8,000 residents and represents a relatively economically homogenous population.[20]

To qualify for OZ designation under the original program, a tract had to meet one of two income-based criteria:

1. median family income less than or equal to 80 percent of the statewide or metropolitan area median income; or
2. a poverty rate of 20 percent or higher.

These thresholds were calculated using the US Census Bureau's American Community Survey (ACS) five-year estimates, specifically data covering 2011 through 2015.[21] The ACS provides a rolling dataset that offers current demographic, social, housing, and economic insights.[22] These tract-level measurements were aligned with the 2010 US Census map, which reflected the most recent boundaries at the time of designation.

Each state governor, along with the mayor of Washington, DC, and the governor of each US territory, was given authority to nominate up to 25 percent of their jurisdiction's eligible low-income census tracts.[23] That 25 percent cap served two purposes: it kept the program targeted and impactful, and it introduced a layer of strategy. Governors had to prioritize which communities to include.

In addition to the core criteria, the original law allowed for a small number of "contiguous tracts" to qualify. These were census

---

20. As of the 2020 US Census, there are over 85,000 census tracts in the United States. The average census tract population is approximately 4,000 residents. "Tallies," The United States Census Bureau, revised July 18, 2022, https://www.census.gov/geographies/reference-files/time-series/geo/tallies.html

21. States were also allowed to use the 2012-2016 ACS dataset to improve tract selection accuracy.

22. "American Community Survey," The United States Census Bureau, last revised January 23, 2026, https://www.census.gov/programs-surveys/acs.html

23. There were a few exceptions to this rule: States with fewer than one hundred eligible tracts were able to designate exactly twenty-five census tracts as Opportunity Zones. States with fewer than twenty-five eligible tracts were able to designate all of their eligible tracts as Opportunity Zones. Puerto Rico was granted a special rule that allowed designation of all 863 of their eligible census tracts as Opportunity Zones.

tracts that didn't meet the low-income requirements themselves but were adjacent to qualifying zones and shared similar characteristics.[24] This rule proved useful for capturing transitional neighborhoods and preserving geographic continuity across zones.

That contiguous tract provision would eventually be eliminated under OZ 2.0, but in the original framework, it allowed for more flexibility in building connected economic geographies.

The New Map for OZ 2.0

Fast forward to 2025, and the Opportunity Zones program has gone from pilot to permanence. But with that permanence comes a critical feature: the map must be redrawn every ten years. Think of it as a cartographic refresh for capital. The framework is written into law for good, but the geographic boundaries are dynamic—updated regularly to ensure the policy stays focused where it's needed most.

Why Redesign the Map at All?

Because Opportunity Zones were never meant to become permanent overlays for already-thriving neighborhoods. The idea was to elevate distressed communities, not lock in benefits for areas that have already rebounded. Without periodic reassessment, OZs risk morphing from a catalyst into an entitlement.

Congress anticipated this. That's why OZ 2.0 includes a built-in cycle: every decade, the census tracts are reviewed, updated, and re-certified using the latest data. It's like pruning a vineyard—done right, it keeps the program healthy and productive.

Here's how the process works.

The redesignation takes place in all years ending in 6, with the new zones taking effect on January 1 of each year ending in 7.

---

24. In order to qualify as a contiguous non-low-income tract, the census tract had to be contiguous with a low-income tract that was designated as a Qualified Opportunity Zone, and the median family income of the tract could not exceed 125 percent of the median family income of the low-income tract with which the tract is contiguous. Additionally, no more than 5 percent of a state's Qualified Opportunity Zones could be contiguous non-low-income tracts.

The first cycle kicks off July 1, 2026, and governors from all fifty states, the governors of US territories, and the mayor of Washington, DC, will have 90 to 120 days to nominate tracts for OZ status.

Those nominations will rely on updated income data[25] from the American Community Survey and will be mapped to the 2020 US Census boundaries. The Treasury Department will then have thirty to sixty days to certify each state's nominations.

The structure of the process mirrors the original framework, but with some key upgrades. First, the eligibility criteria have been tightened.

To be designated under OZ 2.0, a tract must meet one of two income-based tests:

1. median family income less than or equal to 70 percent of the statewide or metropolitan median income; or
2. a poverty rate of 20 percent or higher and a median family income not exceeding 125 percent of the statewide or metropolitan area median.

Additionally, the once-controversial "contiguous tract" provision is gone. Under the original rules, governors could nominate a limited number of tracts that bordered eligible zones, even if they didn't meet the income or poverty thresholds themselves. That door is now closed. Every tract must qualify on its own merits under the tighter OZ 2.0 standards.

For investors, it's not just a bureaucratic shift. It's a clean slate for deploying capital into areas that meet an updated definition of economic distress. For developers, fund managers, and business owners, it's also a strategic reset, a chance to design deals and raise capital aligned with a more focused, reenergized program.

25. The IRS specified in Rev. Proc. 2026-14 that the income data will be sourced from the 2020–2024 American Community Survey (ACS) 5-Year and the 2020 Decennial Census of Island Areas (DECIA) data sets from the Census Bureau.

OZ 1.0 vs. OZ 2.0

	OZ 1.0	OZ 2.0
Enacted	Tax Cuts and Jobs Act (12/22/2017)	One Big Beautiful Bill Act (7/4/2025)
Duration	Temporary Program; Expires 12/31/2026	Permanent with 10-Year Cycles; Starts 1/1/2027
Zone Designation	One-Time on 7/9/2018	Every 10 years, starting 1/1/2027
Zone Expiration	12/31/2028 (12/31/2027 for Puerto Rico's OZ tracts)	Every 10 years, starting 12/31/2036
Zone Eligibility	≤ 80% area/statewide median income; or ≥ 20% poverty rate	≤ 70% area/statewide median income; or ≥ 20% poverty rate + ≤ 125% AMI
Contiguous Zones	Up to 5% non-low-income contiguous	N/A
Number of OZs	8,764	6,544 Anticipated
Reporting	Minimal	Expanded
Gain Deferral	12/31/2026	5 years from date of investment
Gain Reduction (via basis step-ups)	15% for investments by 12/31/2019; 10% for investments by 12/31/2021; none for investments after 2021.	10% applied at 5-year mark of investment.
10-Year Exclusion	OZ investment appreciation is not taxed after achieving a 10-year hold. No depreciation recapture. Step-up to FMV must be taken by 12/31/2047.	OZ investment appreciation is not taxed after achieving a 10-year hold. No depreciation recapture. Step-up to FMV must be taken by 30-year anniversary of investment.
Additional Rural Benefits	N/A	30% basis step-up at 5-year mark; 50% substantial improvement threshold.

OZ 2.0 doesn't replace the Opportunity Zones framework. It modernizes it. The original intent remains intact, but the targeting has improved. The guardrails are tighter. The data is fresher. And if executed well, the impact could be even more meaningful in this second decade.

In other words, the new map is more than a technical update. It's a policy recommitment, an acknowledgment that the program must evolve with economic realities to keep benefits flowing to the communities that still need them most.

"The updated criteria will force developers to be far more deliberate," says Barrett Linburg, co-founder and CEO of Savoy Companies. "The new criteria are stricter, capping income levels and closing loopholes, which will likely result in a materially smaller, more targeted set of eligible tracts."[26]

Scope and Scale of the OZ Program

From the beginning, OZs were a capital formation engine, and the numbers prove it.

Jonathan Tower, founder of Boston-based investment firm Arctaris Impact Investors, was struck by the scale of private dollars mobilized under OZ 1.0. "I was surprised by the sheer volume of disconnected capital that was willing to move once the friction of capital gains tax was removed," he says. "We proved that the private sector is ready to do the work if the incentives are rational."[27]

As of year-end 2023, more than $150 billion[28] in equity had been raised through QOFs, surpassing the Treasury Department's

26. Barrett Linburg (co-founder and CEO of Savoy Companies), via email with the author, January 20, 2026.

27. Jonathan Tower (founder of Arctaris Impact Investors), via email with the author, January 24, 2026.

28. "Opportunity Zone Asset Class Reaches Estimated $150 Billion," OpportunityZones.com, February 14, 2024, https://opportunityzones.com/2024/02/opportunity-zone-asset-class-reaches-estimated-150-billion/

early expectations.[29] But even that impressive figure tells only part of the story.

Zoom in, and you'll find real-world impact across thousands of projects. According to the Economic Innovation Group, Opportunity Zones helped catalyze the creation of over 416,000 new housing units by the first quarter of 2025.[30]

That's not theoretical economic development. That's rooftops, foundations, and front doors.

And it goes far beyond housing. Thousands of Qualified Opportunity Funds (QOFs) and Qualified Opportunity Zone Businesses (QOZBs) have launched nationwide—spanning everything from commercial real estate developments to tech startups and operating companies in manufacturing, clean energy, healthcare, and beyond.

Some projects focus on workforce housing. Others back advanced manufacturing or life sciences facilities. Some fund the restoration of historic buildings or the construction of new infrastructure in disinvested neighborhoods. OZ capital has even flowed into mission-driven business expansions—proof that the program isn't just about real estate.[31]

The scale and creativity of private sector engagement with Opportunity Zones has exceeded expectations, according to Senator Scott. "I've been encouraged to see not only real estate development but also investment in operating businesses, infrastructure, and innovation," he says. "That level of collaboration and initiative confirms that when

---

29. In 2018, Treasury Secretary Steven Mnuchin publicly stated the expectation that "over $100 billion of private capital" would be invested in Opportunity Zones: "Mnuchin expects over $100 billion in opportunity zone investments," OpportunityZones.com, October 1, 2018, https://opportunityzones.com/2018/10/mnuchin-expects-over-100-billion-in-opportunity-zone-investments/

30. Benjamin Glasner, Adam Ozimek, and John Lettieri, "The Impact of Opportunity Zones on Housing Supply," Economic Innovation Group, February 4, 2026, https://eig.org/opportunity-zones-housing-supply/

31. Novogradac's quarterly report on their QOF survey demonstrates that hundreds of millions of OZ dollars have flowed into operating businesses since program inception: Jason Watkins, "At Home in OZs: Novogradac-Tracked QOFs Surpass 200,000 Houses Financed," Novogradac, News and Analysis, July 30, 2025, https://www.novoco.com/notes-from-novogradac/at-home-in-ozs-novogradac-tracked-qofs-surpass-200000-houses-financed

government creates the right incentive and steps back, the private sector can drive meaningful, community-centered growth."[32]

At its core, the Opportunity Zones program was designed for this kind of adaptability. It's scalable, flexible, and it's built for long-term outcomes. Investors can participate through ground-up development, adaptive reuse, business growth, or all of the above.

Because the tax benefits reward patient capital—capital that stays put for ten years—the program naturally attracts investors who are aligned with deeper community outcomes. OZs have become a national laboratory for reimagining how to do community development at scale.

What Constitutes a Valid OZ Investment?

So what exactly makes an OZ investment qualify for these tax benefits? This isn't a free-for-all. There's a structure, and it's essential to understand the basic ingredients before getting into advanced strategy.

There are three core requirements for making a valid, tax-advantaged Opportunity Zone investment.

1. You must first realize a capital gain. This could come from selling stock, real estate, a business, or another appreciated asset.
2. You must reinvest that gain—some or all of it—into a QOF, generally within 180 days.
3. The QOF must invest at least 90 percent of its assets into Qualified Opportunity Zone Property (QOZP).

Let's break that down further. QOZP can take two forms:

- equity interests (stock or partnership interests) in a QOZB—in this structure, a subsidiary entity holds the assets; or
- direct ownership of tangible business property (QOZBP) held by the fund.

32. Tim Scott (US Senator), via email with the author, March 3, 2026.

Each path has its own technical requirements, but the unifying principle is clear: the capital must end up deployed into assets located in Opportunity Zones.

From there, the tax code introduces two important asset-level tests to ensure the program is driving real activity—not just passive investing or speculative land banking. Each qualifying asset must meet one of two tests: it must either qualify as original use property or be substantially improved.

- Original use: The property must be newly placed in service within the OZ. Think ground-up development or a startup business that didn't exist before.
- Substantial improvement: If the investment involves an existing asset (for example, improved real estate), it must be significantly upgraded. Specifically, you must at least double the adjusted basis of the building (excluding land value) over a thirty-month period.[33]

These rules are designed to ensure fresh capital goes toward generating new economic activity in the zone. Think transformation, not stagnation. This program is not for quick flips and speculative land holds; the tax benefits are reserved for investors willing to inject life, value, and equity into underserved neighborhoods.

In the case of QOZBs, there's an additional layer of compliance—things like income-sourcing requirements and limits on "sin businesses," which we'll cover in detail in later chapters.

For now, remember: Opportunity Zones aren't just about geography. They're about *commitment*. The program is built for investors who want to take yesterday's gains and turn them into tomorrow's growth—in places that need it most.

33. As of July 4, 2025 (the date of enactment of the One Big Beautiful Bill Act), the substantial improvement requirement for existing assets located in rural Opportunity Zones was reduced from 100 percent (doubling) to 50 percent.

Common Criticisms and the Evolving Policy Landscape

No federal program of this scale escapes criticism, and OZs were no exception. Almost from the start, questions emerged about who was really benefiting and whether the policy was living up to its promise.

Some of the earliest critiques focused on the zones themselves. A handful of tracts included in the original map were already on an upward trajectory before the policy launched. In those cases, critics argued, OZs weren't catalyzing new investment but rather were subsidizing what was already happening.[34]

Another concern was the program's early lack of transparency. The original law didn't require funds to report standardized impact data to the IRS or any other agency. As a result, it became difficult to track where the money was going or what it was accomplishing. The absence of reliable data created a perception gap: on-the-ground impact was happening in many places, but policymakers and the public couldn't always see it.

Then came the more existential questions.

Were OZs actually helping communities? Were they creating jobs? Raising incomes? Improving access to services? Or were they just fueling gentrification, accelerating displacement, and enriching investors without delivering lasting local benefits?[35]

To their credit, critics raised legitimate issues. But instead of letting the program stall out under pressure, Congress acted. The 2025 passage of the One Big Beautiful Bill Act introduced a suite of structural improvements to the OZ framework, aimed at sharpening focus, increasing accountability, and making the policy more durable.

First, it removed the "contiguous tract" loophole that had allowed higher-income areas to piggyback onto eligible neighborhoods. Now,

---

34. Anjali Kamat, "'Opportunity Zones' Potential Windfall for Developers, Investors," WNYC News, November 6, 2018, https://www.wnyc.org/story/opportunity-zones-potential-windfall-developers-investors/

35. William Fulton, "Opportunity Zones: Gentrification on Steroids?" Kinder Institute for Urban Research, Rice University, February 19, 2019, https://kinder.rice.edu/urbanedge/opportunity-zones-gentrification-steroids

every tract must independently meet the stricter income criteria. That change alone narrows the map and refocuses capital where it's most needed.

Second, it instituted annual impact reporting. QOFs must now submit more robust reporting to the IRS, detailing not just their assets but also measurable outcomes. For the first time, policymakers and the public will get a clear, data-backed view of how OZ capital is being deployed.

Third, the program itself has evolved into something more intentional. OZ 2.0 added tighter guardrails, stronger oversight, and an incentive structure that better aligns with actual community outcomes—not just investor return profiles.

What began as an untested experiment has matured into a more focused, data-driven initiative with bipartisan support and a permanent place in the US tax code. OZs have become less about hype and more about execution.

And that's a good thing.

Why Opportunity Zones Are Stronger Than Ever

Despite early criticism, and maybe because of the reforms it inspired, Opportunity Zones remain one of the most powerful tax incentives in the Internal Revenue Code.

Let's start with the basics. Under OZ 2.0, investors who roll eligible capital gains into a QOF can defer recognition of those gains for five years.[36] That's not just a delay on your tax bill. It's strategic breathing room that lets you reposition your capital.

But the real magic comes in what happens next.

If you hold the investment for at least five years, you receive a 10 percent basis step-up. That means you only owe tax on 90 percent of your original gain. For example, if you roll a $1 million gain into a QOF in 2027 and still hold it in 2032, you'll only recognize $900,000

36. These OZ 2.0 tax benefits apply to any investments made into QOFs after December 31, 2026.

in taxable gain. That 10 percent reduction can create meaningful tax savings—especially for large exits.

Still, that's just the appetizer.

The main course is the ten-year hold. If you keep your investment in the QOF for a full decade, all appreciation is completely excluded from federal capital gains tax. That's right: zero tax on the growth.[37]

Let's say your $1 million investment grows to $3 million by 2037. Under the OZ rules, you pay no tax on the $2 million gain. None. That's not a deferral. That's a permanent exclusion.

And there's more. If your investment includes any depreciated assets, there's no depreciation recapture at exit. That means you can take advantage of accelerated depreciation throughout the hold period—often reducing your taxable income along the way—without paying it back when you sell. It's a rare win-win: immediate tax efficiency plus long-term tax elimination.

Taken together, these benefits form a uniquely compelling trifecta: tax deferral, partial gain reduction, and total exclusion on future upside—with a side of depreciation magic. There's simply nothing else like it in the tax code. And thanks to the One Big Beautiful Bill Act, it's not going away. OZs are now permanent. That clarity gives investors and fund managers the confidence to plan long-term strategies without worrying that the rug will be pulled out from under them.

Perhaps more importantly, though, it signals something bigger: this is no longer a trial run. It's a standing invitation to build wealth—and build communities—with tools that align private return with public benefit.

37. While the Opportunity Zone program is a federal tax incentive, the benefits may apply at the state level as well. The majority of states either have no capital gains tax rate or conform fully or at least partially with the federal incentive. Refer to Appendix C for more information on state-level conformity.

CHAPTER TWO

THE WORLD OF OZ 2.0

WHEN CONGRESS CREATED OPPORTUNITY ZONES in 2017, the idea was both bold and remarkably straightforward: use private capital to breathe life into places too often left behind.

The structure was geographic by design.

The Treasury certified a map of census tracts nominated by governors: neighborhoods, towns, and communities identified as economically distressed. Investors who realized eligible capital gains could roll those gains into Qualified Opportunity Funds (QOFs), which in turn deployed that capital into businesses or real estate within these zones.

A Recap of OZ 1.0

The reward for OZ 1.0 investors was a trio of tax incentives built to favor long-term commitment.

- First, deferral of the original capital gain until December 31, 2026.
- Second, a basis step-up: 10 percent if invested by year-end 2021, 15 percent if in by 2019.[38]
- And third, most powerfully, a complete exclusion of tax on any post-investment appreciation, provided the QOF investment

38. A basis step-up effectively reduces the amount of deferred gain that a taxpayer recognizes in 2026, per IRC § 1400Z-2(b)(2).

was held for at least ten years. That exemption also came with a bonus: no depreciation recapture at exit—a rare feature that made Opportunity Zones stand out even more in a crowded tax-code landscape.

Those were the terms of OZ 1.0. For early movers, the program offered a huge upside.

However, the clock was always ticking.

The policy was temporary by design. OZ 1.0 came with a shrinking runway. By 2022, investors entering the program could still access a deferral and ten-year exclusion, but the other time-based benefits were off the table. There was no basis step-up, and the deferral window was narrowing with each passing year.

The effect was a strange kind of policy fatigue. Some sponsors raced to raise capital before deadlines, while others hesitated to launch new deals with the finish line already looming. The result was that OZ momentum began to cool. The deferral end date, December 31, 2026, wasn't just a statutory line. It had become a psychological one.

And as that deferral date drew nearer, a second act wasn't just possible. It was necessary.

The Second Coming of Opportunity Zones

The most urgent issue was simple: *expiration.*

Opportunity Zones were conceived as a time-limited pilot, a policy test that could be made permanent if it worked. And it did work. The structure catalyzed a wave of early investment. But like a candle designed to burn fast, OZ 1.0 delivered its brightest light early.

By 2022, the signs of slowdown were hard to ignore.

Without a basis step-up and with only a few years of deferral remaining, the math was getting tougher. Fewer investors were willing to begin a ten-year hold without meaningful front-end benefits.

Fewer developers wanted to launch multi-year projects against a hard sunset. That December 31, 2026, date wasn't just a compliance point; it was a psychological ceiling on planning and imagination.[39]

Criticism added pressure. Some of it was fair; some, not so much. A handful of tracts selected under the original 2018 designations were already gentrifying or were on clear upward trajectories. They met the technical eligibility rules, but they didn't align with the public's idea of "distressed." These cases drew media attention. If you were following closely, you might remember the 2019 *New York Times* story that spotlighted a zone in Storey County, Nevada.[40]

The implication: OZs were benefiting the wrong places.

When headlines focus on exceptions, the broader truth gets distorted. Still, perception shapes policy, and the public narrative began to shift.

Lack of transparency didn't help either. OZ 1.0 didn't include robust federal reporting. Policymakers and journalists had to rely on anecdotes and third-party studies, and even advocates for the program were stuck answering basic questions with patchy data:

- How many jobs were created?
- How many new residences were built?
- What businesses got funded?
- What actually happened on the ground?

---

39. This is evident in the QOF equity raising reports that Novogradac produces quarterly. The acceleration of equity raising slowed considerably in 2022, after the 10 percent basis step-up benefit had expired. Jason Watkins, "Novogradac-Tracked QOFs Report More than $1 Billion in Equity Raised in Q2; Ramp-Up in Investment Likely Coming," Novogradac, News and Analysis, July 29, 2025, https://www.novoco.com/notes-from-novogradac/novogradac-tracked-qofs-report-more-than-1-billion-in-equity-raised-in-q2-ramp-up-in-investment-likely-coming

40. Eric Lipton and Jesse Drucker, "Symbol of '80s Greed Stands to Profit From Trump Tax Break for Poor Areas," *New York Times*, October 26, 2019, https://www.nytimes.com/2019/10/26/business/michael-milken-trump-opportunity-zones.html

Those gaps weren't fatal, but they were frustrating. You can't build permanent policy on vibes and case studies.[41]

Then there was the geography problem.

Capital flowed fastest to markets with momentum, often urban areas with existing deal ecosystems, experienced developers, lenders, and advisors. But the policy's original purpose was broader. It was meant to channel capital into persistently distressed communities, where deals are harder, returns can be thinner, and progress takes longer.

On paper, the incentive applied everywhere equally. In reality, some places were simply better equipped to absorb the investment.

Without reform, the OZ pipeline would narrow, and the broader promise of the policy would fade. By late 2022, even experienced sponsors with compelling, community-aligned projects were hesitating. Many feared the window would close before their capital stacks came together.

Investors and developers weren't asking for special treatment. They were asking for stability: a durable, forward-looking framework they could plan around.

That's what OZ 2.0 aimed to deliver: extend the horizon, sharpen the targeting, and bring accountability into focus.

Policy Rationale for OZ 2.0

The case for reform didn't begin with complaints. It began with evidence. OZ 1.0 worked.[42]

---

41. In the previous chapter, I cited an EIG study that reported over 416,000 new housing units created by Opportunity Zones. Another smaller study looks at housing units produced by one developer: Capital Square is in the process of developing 2,000 residential units across nine different OZ projects as of November 2024. Jimmy Atkinson, "Capital Square's 2,000 New OZ Housing Units, With Louis Rogers & Whit Huffman" OpportunityZones.com, November 25, 2024, https://opportunityzones.com/2024/11/louis-rogers-whit-huffman-324/

42. According to an EIG research brief, by the end of 2020, OZ investment had reached at least $48 billion in equity, across nearly half of all designated communities. Kenan Fikri et al., "Examining the Latest Multi-Year Evidence on the Scale and Effects of Opportunity Zones Investment," Economic Innovation Group, EIG Brief, March 22, 2023, https://eig.org/wp-content/uploads/2023/03/Examining-the-Latest-Multi-Year-Evidence-on-Opportunity-Zones-Investment.pdf

Capital moved. Projects were built in places that hadn't seen cranes or ribbon cuttings in decades. Operating businesses raised equity, and jobs followed. Even without a centralized data system, the aggregate picture was hard to ignore: the program was working.

"I've been surprised by how often the intent of Congress actually played out on the ground," says Barrett Linburg, co-founder and CEO of Savoy Companies.

Linburg leads a vertically integrated multifamily real estate platform based in Dallas, Texas, that is developing several hundred units in the city's Bishop Ridge neighborhood, largely with OZ capital.

"In the Bishop Ridge neighborhood of Dallas, we didn't just buy a building," says Linburg. "We aggregated fifteen distressed properties comprising over 400 units and are now delivering nearly 300 new mixed-income apartments, the first new construction that neighborhood has seen in half a century. That is exactly what patient, place-based capital was designed to do: go where other capital wouldn't."[43]

Not only was it working; it was popular. Sponsors, investors, and local officials all leaned in. The incentive had traction. But popularity alone isn't enough to sustain a federal program. Durability requires credibility. That meant acknowledging weak spots and evolving the policy without losing what made it powerful in the first place.

First up: census tract eligibility tightening. If a few tracts felt like they missed the mark—too affluent, too far from distress—then raise the bar. Update the map using fresher data and a more rigorous filter.

Second: reporting. Policymakers needed real-time feedback loops. If you can't measure outcomes, you can't justify the program. So OZ 2.0 includes a new federal reporting mandate for QOFs, and it creates a structured way to capture results: housing units delivered, jobs supported, businesses funded. And an annual report

---

43. Barrett Linburg (co-founder and CEO of Savoy Companies), via email with the author, January 20, 2026.

from the Treasury Department to the American public. No more guesswork.[44]

Third: targeted support for overlooked markets. Rural communities, in particular, faced structural disadvantages under OZ 1.0. They had fewer shovel-ready projects, smaller developer networks, and often lacked the infrastructure necessary to participate. If OZ 1.0 left them behind, OZ 2.0 gave them a running start—with better terms and a lower bar for participation.

And then there was timing.

The 2026 sunset baked into OZ 1.0 wasn't just an accounting deadline—it was a legislative spark. As the date approached, it aligned perfectly with a broader moment: the expiration of other major provisions in the 2017 Tax Cuts and Jobs Act.

Washington was already preparing for a tax reset. OZ advocates saw the opportunity: position reform not as a one-off, but as part of a broader, Republican-backed tax package. The timing couldn't have been better. Investors were asking for clarity. Communities were ready. The program had a track record. What it needed now was a path to permanence.

The solution came in 2024, and it was big.

One Big Election, One Big Bill

Every four years, American politics stages its favorite drama: a high-stakes, coast-to-coast production with familiar characters, surprise twists, and real consequences.

Still, the 2024 election felt different.

The country wasn't just choosing between two presidential candidates; it was staring down inflation, market uncertainty, and a tax

---

44. The Treasury Department will take the information reported by QOFs to issue an annual report on Opportunity Zones that will include the total number of QOFs, the aggregate dollar amount held by QOFs, the types of businesses receiving QOF investment, the number of new residential units created by QOFs, and a breakdown of data by census tract.

code packed with soon-to-expire tax cuts from Trump's first term.[45] The economy took center stage, and voters knew the outcome would shape everything from interest rates to investment policy.[46]

When the ballots were counted, the results delivered clarity. Donald Trump reclaimed the White House, and Republicans held their majority in the House and flipped the Senate. It was a clean sweep, and it gave the GOP a clear runway to act fast on its tax agenda.

Opportunity Zones had been waiting in the wings.

The program was always meant to be revisited, and by 2025, that moment had arrived. The incentive was nearing its sunset, and many of the TCJA's core provisions were set to expire within two years. OZ reform didn't need its own spotlight; it needed a ride on something moving big and fast.

That vehicle was the sweeping reconciliation package quickly dubbed the One Big Beautiful Bill Act. A nod to Trump's signature flair, the legislation stitched together extensions of the TCJA, renewing numerous tax incentives, including Opportunity Zones.

This wasn't a lucky break, though.

The OZ industry had been laying the groundwork for years. Sponsors brought forward track records. Community leaders highlighted impact. Industry advocates met with lawmakers and staff, armed with data and outcomes, not just theory.[47] The pitch was clear: Opportunity Zones worked, but they needed more time, better targeting, and increased accountability.

---

45. Margot Crandall-Hollick and Joseph Rosenberg, "Unpacking the TCJA: Who Benefits and Who Loses from Extending Major Provisions," Tax Policy Center, Urban Institute & Brookings Institution, December 19, 2024, https://taxpolicycenter.org/taxvox/unpacking-tcja-who-benefits-and-who-loses-extending-major-provisions

46. "Issues and the 2024 Election," Pew Research Center, September 9, 2024, https://www.pewresearch.org/politics/2024/09/09/issues-and-the-2024-election/

47. For my part, I rallied members of my OZ Insiders mastermind group and my audience at OpportunityZones.com to sign an advocacy letter. Many of the suggestions in our letter were ultimately adopted into law: https://opportunityzones.com/wp-content/uploads/2025/06/OZ-2.0-Legislation-Support-Letter-2025.pdf

When the bill sprinted through Congress and hit the President's desk on July 4, 2025, it marked more than a policy win. It was a statement. OZs weren't going away; they were growing up. Permanence was no longer an ambition.

It was the law.

And just like that, the rules changed. Investors stopped racing against deadlines and started thinking in decades. Developers revisited strategies that once seemed impossible. The second era of Opportunity Zones had officially begun.

What OZ 2.0 Does

The headline change is simple: *permanence.*

OZs are no longer tied to an expiration date. That alone rewrites the playbook. Without a sunset date looming, multi-phase projects make more sense. Long-dated business plans are easier to model. Investors aren't racing a calendar; they're building for the long haul.

"The importance of permanency of the OZ incentive cannot be overstated," says Michael Novogradac, managing partner at Novogradac & Company LLP.[48]

OZ 1.0 was a game changer, but not everyone utilized it to its full potential. Many local stakeholders were dissuaded because of its temporary nature.

"In the early years of OZs, many community development professionals took a look, saw the community development potential, and embraced OZs," says Novogradac. "Others saw the incentive as a temporary pilot program, didn't immediately identify ways to use the incentive to further their mission, and didn't pursue OZ opportunities."[49]

OZ permanence gives local stakeholders more confidence in the program's longevity and ensures that existing projects aren't abandoned prematurely.

---

48. Michael Novogradac (managing partner at Novogradac & Company LLP), via email with the author, January 8, 2026.

49. Ibid.

According to US Representative Mike Kelly (R-PA), Chairman of the Ways and Means Subcommittee on Tax, "For communities and investors alike, the expanded Opportunity Zones program means certainty. Without the extension of the OZ program, it was quite possible that existing projects and funding could have stopped altogether."[50]

Permanence, however, is just the beginning. OZ 2.0 brings a suite of enhancements that sharpen the original vision while fixing some of its blind spots.

The map is getting a refresh. Starting January 1, 2027, a new set of tracts—nominated by governors and selected using updated income data—will define the next decade of eligible zones. The nomination process is still place-based, but the bar is higher. Contiguous tracts are out. The focus is squarely on genuine economic distress. And the map will now be updated every ten years, ensuring stability of the program and alignment with evolving needs.

"Making Opportunity Zones permanent gives both communities and investors the certainty they have been missing," says US Representative Jason Smith (R-MO), chairman of the Ways and Means Committee. "Instead of a sunset date that discouraged long-term commitments, now businesses, developers, and local leaders can plan ten, fifteen, even twenty years into the future knowing these incentives are not going away."[51]

The investor side remains anchored by the ten-year hold benefit. As before, if you invest through a QOF and hold for at least a decade, all post-investment appreciation is exempt from capital gains tax.[52] No depreciation recapture, no capital gains on exit. That remains the crown jewel of the program.

What's new is the deferral schedule.

---

50. Kelly, email.

51. Jason Smith (US Representative), via email with the author, January 9, 2026.

52. One new component to the ten-year benefit is the requirement to take it within thirty years. If a QOF investment is still held at the thirty-year anniversary of investment, a step-up to fair market value is taken at that time. Any appreciation thereafter is taxable.

For post-2026 investments, gain deferral isn't pegged to December 31, 2026, anymore. It starts on your investment date and lasts five years. After that, the deferred gain is recognized—minus a 10 percent basis step-up if you've held the investment for at least five years by that point. (I'll address tax deferrals more in depth in Chapter 3.)

For rural investments, the incentive gets even better. Investments in Qualified Rural Opportunity Funds (QROFs) receive a 30 percent basis step-up on the deferred gain and face a reduced substantial improvement threshold for improvements to existing assets. That makes rehab and reuse in smaller markets far more viable. This rural targeting is one of OZ 2.0's most deliberate recalibrations, because in OZ 1.0, rural communities received relatively little investment.

According to Jill Homan, deputy director of trade and economic policy at the America First Policy Institute, "While rural Opportunity Zones were proportionately designated relative to the number of rural census tracts (about 24 percent), these rural OZs ended up receiving less investment compared to their proportion of the country. Only about 9 percent of the OZ investment was in rural OZs compared to non-rural OZs."[53]

Transparency also gets a major upgrade.

Beginning in tax year 2026, QOFs are required to report on metrics that go beyond dollars raised: job creation, housing units built, NAICS codes, and other tangible impact indicators. This data will be compiled into annual Treasury reports, giving the public—and policymakers—a clear view of where OZ capital is flowing and what it's producing.

Taken together, OZ 2.0 is more than a policy tweak. It's a full reboot.

Rep. Smith says, "Opportunity Zones 2.0 locks in and builds on the success of the OZ program created in the 2017 Trump tax cuts.

---

53. Jill Homan (deputy director of trade and economic policy at the America First Policy Institute), via email with the author, January 9, 2026.

The 2017 version was a major policy innovation, and we have now had the chance to see what worked best and what could be adjusted to enhance the program further."[54]

With a stable foundation, a cleaner map, stronger incentives for rural America, and more robust reporting mechanisms, the second era of Opportunity Zones isn't just longer; it's smarter.

OZ 2.0 Effective Dates and Key Deadlines

Every OZ stakeholder—investors, fund managers, community leaders—experiences OZ 2.0 through a different lens. But the common thread is timing. Knowing the key dates can be the difference between a compliant investment and a missed opportunity.

1. KEY DATES FOR INVESTORS

The biggest dividing line is December 31, 2026. Investments of eligible gains *after* that date fall under OZ 2.0's updated rules: notably a five-year deferral and a 10 percent basis step-up (30 percent for investments into rural areas).

If you can control when to trigger gains, timing becomes strategy. Gains realized on or after July 6, 2026, under the standard 180-day rule can be invested in 2027 and therefore qualify for new OZ 2.0 benefits. That alignment can make a material difference to after-tax outcomes.

Investors with pass-through entity gains reported to them via a Schedule K-1[55] have even more flexibility. These taxpayers can elect to start the 180-day clock from three points: the realization date, the end of the tax year (usually December 31), or the due date of the passthrough entity's tax return (typically March 15 of the following

54. Smith, email.

55. Schedules K-1 are typically issued to members of partnerships, multi-member LLCs, and S-corps. Estates and trusts may issue them to beneficiaries. Some Limited Partnership, Master Limited Partnerships, private equity funds, and specialty ETFs may also issue K-1s to investors.

year). Using the December 31 or March 15 option allows OZ 2.0 investments well into the following year.[56]

The takeaway: if you want the revised deferral structure or rural incentives, map your gain realization date carefully. The ten-year appreciation exclusion remains the marquee benefit, but the entry mechanics are where the leverage lives.

2. KEY DATES FOR QOFs

For Qualified Opportunity Funds, OZ 2.0's clock started ticking on July 4, 2025—the day the law was signed and the substantial improvement threshold for rural projects dropped from 100 percent to 50 percent. That change applied at the date of enactment and opened new deal types in rural markets that previously didn't pencil.

The next milestone was January 1, 2026, when mandatory reporting kicked in. QOFs now must begin tracking specific data sets, including:

- employee counts;
- NAICS classifications; and
- new housing units tied to fund activity.

The first reporting deadline is March 2027, when 2026 tax returns are due for QOFs.

It is also important to note the dual-map period from January 1, 2027, to December 31, 2028. During this two-year window, investors may be able to deploy capital into both retiring OZ 1.0 tracts and new OZ 2.0 tracts.[57]

---

56. Technically, the 180-day clock on a gain realized by a passthrough entity as early as January 1, 2026, and subsequently reported via a Schedule K-1 can start as late as March 15, 2027. In this example, the member of the entity receiving the K-1 has until September 10, 2027 to defer the gain into a QOF. And in this example, the gain (although realized in 2026) is eligible for the OZ 2.0 tax benefits if invested into a QOF in 2027.

57. This dual-map period exists because the new OZ 2.0 zones will go into effect on January 1, 2027. But the old OZ 1.0 zones don't expire until December 31, 2028, per the Tax Cuts and Jobs Act. Per IRS Rev. Proc. 2026-14, Puerto Rico's OZ 1.0 zones expire December 31, 2027. As of the writing of this book, it is believed that OZ 2.0 dollars that fund QOFs after 2026 may be deployed into projects in OZ 1.0 tracts, unless future IRS regulations expressly prohibit this.

3. KEY DATES FOR NEW OPPORTUNITY ZONE DESIGNATIONS

With OZ 2.0, the map isn't static; it's scheduled. Every ten years, a fresh designation process redraws the boundaries.

Here's the site selection process for OZ 2.0.

- Determination period: Effective July 1, 2026, states and territories have up to ninety days to nominate a new round of Opportunity Zones based on updated income data and tighter criteria. That window can be extended once, for an additional thirty days. The governor of each state and inhabited overseas territory, plus the mayor of Washington, DC, can nominate up to 25 percent of their eligible low-income census tracts.[58] With the "contiguous tract" loophole gone, each nomination must stand on its own data, making the competition for designation fierce.
- Consideration period: Once nominations are in, the Treasury Department has thirty to sixty days to review and certify the zones.
- Map effective date: The new OZ 2.0 map is effective on January 1, 2027. At that point, both the new and old zones will be active for a two-year overlap—a bridge that may allow investors and developers to operate across both maps simultaneously.
- Expiration of OZ 2.0 Designation: OZ 2.0 tracts are certified for ten years, expiring on December 31, 2036. After that, the process begins again: nominations in 2036, new zones effective January 1, 2037.
- Repeating cycle: After the 2036 sunset, the same designation sequence repeats for the next round of zones every ten years. New zones are nominated and certified in the second half of

58. As in OZ 1.0, there is an exception to this rule: Jurisdictions with fewer than one hundred eligible tracts are able to designate exactly twenty-five census tracts as Opportunity Zones. Jurisdictions with fewer than twenty-five eligible tracts are able to designate all of their eligible tracts as Opportunity Zones. The special rule that allowed Puerto Rico to designate all of their low-income tracts as OZs in 2018 no longer exists for subsequent designation rounds.

all years that end in 6. And those new zones take effect on January 1 in all years ending in 7.

This rolling structure gives the program rhythm. It keeps the policy fresh and focused and gives communities a once-per-decade opportunity to compete for investment-ready designation.

Transition Planning for Investors and Developers

With the dates in place, strategy comes into view. OZ 2.0 isn't just about new rules; it's also about sequencing, positioning, and readiness.

For investors, especially those with control over when to recognize gains, timing is leverage.

Want to qualify for the new five-year deferral and 10 percent basis step-up under OZ 2.0? Your eligible gain needs to be reinvested *after* December 31, 2026. That means working backward. If you realize a gain on or after July 6, 2026, you've got a full 180-day window that takes you into the first half of 2027—comfortably within OZ 2.0 territory.[59] This is more than tax timing; it's portfolio engineering. The ten-year hold is still the keystone, but your entry point shapes how much you actually keep.

For developers and sponsors, the dual-map period (2027–2028) is an invitation to potentially run a two-track strategy. Investors have two years where the OZ 1.0 and OZ 2.0 maps will overlap—plenty of time to complete construction, lease up, or stabilize OZ 1.0 projects, even as you lock in land and entitlements for OZ 2.0 zones coming online.

The most competitive funds will treat reporting not as a burden, but as proof of performance—evidence that can differentiate them in a crowded capital market.

For rural-focused investors and developers, the policy has turned in your favor. The 30 percent rural basis step-up and the reduced 50 percent substantial improvement threshold fundamentally change

---

59. As previously mentioned, gains reported on a Schedule K-1 can be realized at any point in 2026 and still be eligible for OZ 2.0 investment in 2027.

the math in smaller markets. Projects that once sat on the edge of viability—small-town adaptive reuse, modest multifamily rehabs, local operating businesses—may now clear the bar.

If you've been building in these markets already but are hesitant to embrace the OZ incentive as a strategy, now is the time to revisit your models.

OZ 2.0 doesn't just reward patience; it rewards presence.

CHAPTER THREE

OZ TAX ADVANTAGE AND TIMING RULES

BEFORE WE GET INTO ADVANCED STRATEGIES, you need to know how the engine works.

Opportunity Zones are powerful, but only if you understand how and when to use them. This chapter walks you through the key mechanics of OZ 2.0: the benefits, the timing rules, and the compliance framework that underpins it all.

Think of this as the rulebook.

Without it, you're flying blind, and there's no amount of clever structuring or sharp investing that can save you from missing a deadline or misunderstanding a holding period. I've seen sophisticated investors—and even fund managers—lose six or seven figures in tax savings because of simple missteps.

The goal here is to make sure that doesn't happen to you. By the end of this chapter, you'll be able to:

1. identify and apply the four core OZ 2.0 tax benefits;
2. understand the timing rules that control eligibility; and
3. avoid the most common mistakes that trigger penalties or disqualification.

Let's be clear: these benefits are earned. They're conditional. You don't get a second shot if you miss your 180-day window. You don't get to claim tax-free appreciation if you sell in year nine. This is a compliance-heavy program, and that's by design.

That said, once you understand the rules, they're not impossible to follow. In fact, many of them mirror the rhythms of a well-run investment process: commit long-term, plan your capital deployment, and manage your deadlines.

The challenge isn't complexity; it's discipline, which means you need to have a practical mindset. How will you structure your next investment? How will you manage timing across multiple partners or entities? How will you build your compliance process so that tax strategy doesn't become a liability?

This isn't just theoretical. You'll need to keep one eye on the calendar and one eye on the investment thesis at all times.

In the next chapter, we'll move from the what to the who. We'll explore which investors benefit most from OZs, how to determine if this fits into your strategy, and where OZs are a mismatch. But for now, don't skip ahead. Master the details in this chapter first because everything else builds on this.

The Four Core OZ Tax Benefits (OZ 2.0)

Opportunity Zones 2.0 offers four tax benefits. Each is powerful on its own, but the real value comes when you stack them—structuring your investment to take advantage of all four.

1. DEFERRAL OF ELIGIBLE GAINS

The first benefit is immediate: when you reinvest eligible capital gains into a Qualified Opportunity Fund (QOF), you can defer the tax on those gains. Under OZ 2.0, the deferral lasts five years from the date of investment—no matter when that investment is made.

This is a major departure from OZ 1.0, where deferral ended on a fixed date (December 31, 2026), regardless of when you entered the program. Starting January 1, 2027, each investor gets a rolling five-year window. That means more capital at work longer, compounding inside the QOF for longer.

2. REDUCTION OF DEFERRED GAIN

Next, OZ 2.0 gives you a basis step-up on your QOF investment, thereby reducing the amount of deferred gain that you recognize at the five-year mark. For most investments, that step-up is 10 percent—meaning you'll only pay tax on 90 percent of your original gain. If your QOF qualifies as a Qualified Rural Opportunity Fund (QROF), the benefit is even better: a 30 percent step-up means you'll only pay tax on 70 percent of your original gain.

That's not just a deferral; it's a discount. You're locking in a reduction in your future tax bill, just for being an Opportunity Zone investor.[60]

3. PERMANENT EXCLUSION OF POST-INVESTMENT APPRECIATION

This is the heart of the program. If you hold your QOF investment for at least ten years, you can exclude all post-investment appreciation from federal capital gains tax. Sell for double, triple, or more—your entire gain is tax-free.

There's no ceiling here. The bigger your asset grows, the bigger the benefit. That's why OZ investing is often described as the ultimate reward for patient capital.

Note: OZ appreciation isn't tax-free forever. At the thirty-year mark, you must elect a step-up to fair market value. Gains above that point are taxable, which means your tax-free window has a defined endpoint.

---

60. While the amount of gain recognized is reduced by 10 percent (or 30 percent for rural investments), the reader should note that the tax rate that applies is the capital gains tax rate in the year in which the deferred gain is recognized. Therefore, it's not guaranteed that the tax bill itself will be reduced, as there's a risk that the capital gains tax rate will increase in the future. Such an increase would lessen the impact of the first two benefits, but it would make the third benefit (permanent exclusion of post-investment appreciation) more impactful.

Comparing After-Tax Returns: Non-OZ vs. Opportunity Zone Investing

	Non-OZ Investment	OZ Investment
Initial Gain	$1,000,000	$1,000,000
Tax on Gain	($238,000)	Deferred
After-Tax Investable Amount	$762,000	$1,000,000
10-Year Equity Multiple	2.5x	2.5x
Value After 10 Years	$1,905,000	$2,500,000
Total Appreciation	$1,143,000	$1,500,000
Tax on Appreciation	($272,034)	$0
Deferred Gain Recognized (Year 5)	$0	$900,000
Tax on Deferred Gain (Year 5)	$0	($214,200)
Ending After-Tax Value	**$1,632,966**	**$2,285,800**
After-Tax OZ Advantage	–	**+$652,834 (+40%)**

Assumes a post-2026 non-rural OZ 2.0 investment of a $1,000,000 eligible long-term capital gain deferred into a Qualified Opportunity Fund, held for 10 years, with a 10% basis step-up after 5 years and a 23.8% federal capital gains tax rate in both the year of the initial gain and the year in which the deferral ends. Ignores interim cash distributions, depreciation benefits, and possible state tax effects. In this example, the OZ investor ends with approximately 40% more after-tax wealth on the same original gain.

4. NO DEPRECIATION RECAPTURE

This is one of the most underappreciated benefits. Ordinarily, when you sell a depreciated asset, the IRS claws back the depreciation as recaptured income.

In OZs, if you hit the ten-year hold, that recapture disappears. You keep all the depreciation you've taken over the holding period, tax-free. It's a major advantage for real estate and other asset-heavy investments—allowing you to maximize tax-sheltered cash flow during the hold and exit clean on the back end. Utilizing a cost segregation study in the early years of the project compounds this benefit.

A Technical Example: How the Four OZ Benefits Work Together

Let's see how these benefits work in the real world. This section is a bit more technical, but bear with me, as it shows the power of the OZ benefits in action.

Suppose Mike, an American taxpayer, sells stock on August 1, 2026, for $1,250,000. His cost basis is $250,000, which results in a capital gain of $1,000,000, with $238,000[61] owed to Uncle Sam. Mike reinvests that full $1,000,000 gain into a QOF on January 15, 2027.[62] The investment qualifies for OZ treatment because it falls within the 180-day window.[63]

Over the next thirteen years, the QOF holds assets that depreciate—and that depreciation flows through to the investor, offsetting passive income. Then, on December 1, 2039, the QOF exits its investment and distributes $2,500,000 back to the Mike, reflecting a $1,500,000 gain.

Here's how the four OZ benefits apply:

1. DEFERRAL OF ELIGIBLE GAINS

Mike's $1,000,000 gain is deferred for five years—from January 15, 2027, to January 15, 2032. The tax on this gain is due April 15, 2033,[64] with the filing of his 2032 return.[65]

---

61. Assuming a federal capital gains tax rate of 20 percent, plus a 3.8 percent net investment income tax rate.

62. The investment on this date is timely, because the 180-day window for this eligible gain runs from August 1, 2026, through January 27, 2027. And because the taxpayer is making an investment after December 31, 2026, the OZ 2.0 benefits apply.

63. Note that only the gain amount (not the entire proceeds from the transaction) is eligible for favorable tax treatment. In our example, the taxpayer invested his entire gain into a QOF, but he could have also invested just a portion of the gain. Only the portion invested in a QOF is eligible for OZ tax treatment.

64. Quarterly estimated payments may be due earlier than this.

65. Of note, the tax rate in the year of recognition is the applicable tax rate. In our example, the 2032 tax rate would apply to the deferred gain. Also, the characterization of the gain (short-term or long-term) is retained.

2. REDUCTION OF DEFERRED GAIN

Thanks to OZ 2.0, Mike qualifies for a 10 percent basis step-up. So instead of recognizing the full $1,000,000 gain, he only reports $900,000, erasing $100,000 from his taxable gain.[66] (Note: if this had been a QROF investment, the reduction would be 30 percent, meaning only $700,000 would be taxable.)

3. PERMANENT EXCLUSION OF POST-INVESTMENT APPRECIATION

Because Mike holds his QOF investment for more than ten years, the full $1,500,000 gain from the sale in 2039 is excluded from federal capital gains tax. As a result, Mike owes nothing to Uncle Sam. *Nada.*

4. NO DEPRECIATION RECAPTURE

Over those thirteen years, the QOF passed through depreciation to its investors; often as much as 50 to 70 percent[67] of the original investment is depreciated. Normally, that would trigger depreciation recapture at the time of sale. But since this was a qualifying OZ investment held over ten years, that recapture is waived.

This example illustrates the layered power of OZ 2.0. Each benefit adds to the last, building toward a dramatically more favorable after-tax outcome. But remember: every advantage shown here is earned by hitting specific deadlines and holding periods.

Next, we'll explore what kinds of gains actually qualify—because not every dollar you earn is eligible for this treatment.

Let's break down the rules.

---

66. The amount of gain recognized at the deferral date is typically 90 percent of the gain invested in a QOF. In our example, $900,000 instead of $1,000,000. But in the case of an investment in a Qualified Rural Opportunity Fund (QROF), the taxpayer is granted a 30 percent basis step-up, which reduces his gain by 30 percent. In our example, the taxpayer's $1,000,000 gain would be reduced to $700,000. Further, per IRC § 1400Z-2(b)(2)(A), the amount of gain recognized on the deferral date is limited by the fair market value of the taxpayer's investment on that date.

67. This "50 to 70 percent" figure after thirteen years assumes a cost segregation study is performed, resulting in 20 to 25 percent bonus depreciation in just the first year.

Eligible Gains: What Qualifies

Not all capital is created equal. The Opportunity Zone incentive is generous, but it is also precise. If your dollars don't meet the test, they won't qualify for the tax benefits.

The IRS makes this clear: *only capital gains recognized for federal income tax purposes can be rolled over into a Qualified Opportunity Fund.*[68] That means no ordinary income, no borrowed funds, no savings. You must have realized a capital gain, and you must invest it within the rules.

TYPES OF GAINS THAT QUALIFY

Eligible gains can come from a wide range of sources, including (but not limited to):

- public market securities: gains from selling stocks, bonds, mutual funds, or ETFs;
- real estate: gains from selling investment property, business-use property, second homes, vacation homes, or a primary residence (to the extent it exceeds the exclusion);[69]
- business or partnership sales: gains from selling all or part of an operating business, business assets, or partnership interests;
- collectibles: gains from selling art, classic cars, comic books, baseball cards, or other capital assets categorized as collectibles; and
- crypto assets: gains from selling digital assets like Bitcoin, Ethereum, or other cryptocurrencies.

The common denominator: these gains must be recognized for federal tax purposes and meet the definition of a capital gain. That's true whether the gain is short-term or long-term.

---

68. "Invest in a Qualified Opportunity Fund," Internal Revenue Service, US Department of the Treasury, https://www.irs.gov/credits-deductions/businesses/invest-in-a-qualified-opportunity-fund

69. The IRC § 121 exclusion allows qualifying homeowners to exclude up to $250,000 of gain from the sale of their primary residence (up to $500,000 for married couples filing jointly).

WHAT DOESN'T QUALIFY

Just as important is what doesn't make the cut:

- non-gain dollars: you can invest ordinary income or savings into an Opportunity Zone project, but they won't qualify for OZ tax benefits;
- recaptured gains: Section 1245 and 1250 recaptured gains are typically ineligible; and
- related-party transactions: gains from selling to related parties are explicitly disqualified.[70]

Missing these distinctions can cost you the entire benefit. Don't assume a gain is eligible; know it is before you invest.

The 180-Day Rule

Every Opportunity Zone investment starts with a countdown.

From the moment you recognize a capital gain, you typically have 180 days to reinvest that gain (or part of it) into a QOF.[71] Miss that window, and the tax benefit is lost—permanently.

THE GENERAL RULE

For most investors, the 180-day clock starts on the date the gain is realized. For example, if you realize a gain on August 1, you have until January 27 of the following year to reinvest it. Although it's straightforward enough, that's just the beginning. Certain types of gains offer more flexibility—particularly gains from passthrough entities.

Here's the breakdown.

---

70. Per IRC § 1400Z-2(e)(2), "related parties" for Opportunity Zones are defined by substituting a 20 percent threshold into IRC §§ 267(b) and 707(b)(1).

71. IRC § 1400Z-2(a)(1)(A)

PASSTHROUGH ENTITY GAINS

If your gain comes through a partnership, multi-member LLC, S corporation, or a regarded trust, and is reported on a Schedule K-1, you have three options for starting your 180-day clock:[72]

1. the date of the sale that triggered the gain;
2. the last day of the entity's tax year, typically December 31; or
3. the due date of the entity's tax return (without extensions), typically March 15 of the following year.

For example, one of Mike's partnerships realized a gain on January 15, 2026, and he decided to take his share of the gain and invest it into a QOF.

Using option 1 above, Mike would have 180 days starting on January 15, 2026, making his deadline for investing the gain into a QOF July 13, 2026.

Using option 2 above, he has 180 days starting December 31, 2026, assuming the entity's tax year is tied to the calendar year, making his deadline June 28, 2027.

Finally, using option 3 above, Mike has 180 days starting March 15, 2027, making his deadline September 10, 2027.

This flexibility can be a lifesaver if the original sale date occurred several months prior and you need more time to identify and fund an OZ investment.

INSTALLMENT SALES

If your gain is part of an installment sale,[73] you get to choose:

1. starting a single 180-day window from the *last day of the tax year* in which the sale occurred; or
2. starting a *separate 180-day window* from the date of *each payment* received.

---

72. Treas. Reg. § 1.1400Z2(a)-1(c)(8)(iii)
73. Treas. Reg. § 1.1400Z2(a)-1(b)(11)(viii)(B)

This flexibility allows you to align your reinvestment window with the actual arrival of cash, but only if you understand and apply the rule correctly.

SECTION 1231 GAINS

If your gain comes from selling business-use property (known as Section 1231 gains), you can elect to start your 180-day period on the last day of the tax year.[74] That can buy you time to identify a QOF and deploy capital strategically.

WHY IT MATTERS

The 180-day rule is one of the *most common points of failure* in OZ compliance. Miss your window, and the IRS will treat your investment as a non-qualified contribution. No deferral. No exclusion. No do-over. The takeaway: know your gain type, understand the rules that apply, and coordinate with a tax advisor early before your reinvestment clock even starts ticking.

Key Holding Period Milestones (OZ 2.0)

Once your investment is in a QOF, the clock doesn't stop. It shifts to a longer game, where timing determines how much benefit you actually unlock.

Under OZ 2.0, there are three critical milestones: five years, ten years, and thirty years.

THE FIVE-YEAR MILESTONE: END OF DEFERRAL

At the five-year mark from your investment date, your original gain becomes taxable.

This is when the IRS officially recognizes the gain you rolled over, but only after reducing the original gain by the basis step-up: 10 percent for standard QOFs and 30 percent for Qualified Rural Opportunity Funds (QROFs).

---

74. Treas. Reg. § 1.1400Z2(a)-1(b)(11)(iii)(B)

That's a key shift from OZ 1.0. Previously, deferral always ended on December 31, 2026 (absent an inclusion event that would cause the deferred gain to be recognized prior to that date). Under OZ 2.0, every investor gets a five-year deferral from the moment of investment, regardless of when they enter the program. It makes the value of this benefit much more durable compared to the original program. And in fact, of all the new OZ improvements contained in the One Big Beautiful Bill Act, the five-year deferral is the most popular one.[75]

"People love that rolling five-year deferral," says Ashley Tison, president of OZPros. "As a result, this will make Opportunity Zones more ubiquitous in people's tax mitigation toolkit. There's something psychological about writing a check to the government. If people can delay that for five years, they're all over it."[76]

THE TEN-YEAR MILESTONE: PERMANENT EXCLUSION

The most valuable benefit, the ten-year exclusion, remained intact from OZ 1.0.

And this is the big one.

If you hold your QOF investment for at least ten years, you get a *complete* federal capital gains tax exclusion on any appreciation. No matter how much your asset grows in value, that growth is *never* taxed.

This is why OZs are often called the best long-term tax play in the code; it's not just deferring tax, it's *erasing* it on all post-investment gains.

THE THIRTY-YEAR MILESTONE: STEP-UP TO FAIR MARKET VALUE

The Opportunity Zone benefits don't accrue forever. At the thirty-year anniversary of your QOF investment, you're required to sell or take a step-up in basis to fair market value.[77]

---

75. "2025 Opportunity Zones Survey Reveals Strong Excitement For OZ 2.0," OpportunityZones.com., December 12, 2025, https://opportunityzones.com/2025/12/2025-opportunity-zones-survey/

76. Ashley Tison (president of OZPros), phone interview with the author, January 20, 2026.

77. This thirty-year limit is codified in IRC § 1400Z-2(c)(A), effective for OZ 2.0 investments on or after January 1, 2027. Previously (under OZ 1.0), the limit was defined as December 31, 2047 in Treas. Reg. § 1.1400Z2(c)-1(c).

This locks in your tax-free appreciation.

Any further gains above that stepped-up value—if you continue holding the asset—are taxable. But thirty years is a long runway for compounding, harvesting tax-free returns, or planning your exit strategy.

CONTINUOUS INVESTMENT REQUIRED

To earn these benefits, you must maintain a continuous investment in the QOF. Selling, even partially, before hitting the five- or ten-year milestones triggers recognition of gain and may cancel eligibility for key benefits.

This is a program for committed capital. It rewards investors who can stay the course.

Of course, favorable holding periods alone do not guarantee Opportunity Zone benefits. Those tax advantages remain contingent on the QOF and its underlying assets satisfying the program's ongoing compliance requirements.

The Thirty-Month Substantial Improvement Rule

If your QOF holds existing tangible property in an Opportunity Zone, merely owning it isn't enough to qualify for the tax benefits. Unless the property satisfies the original use standard, you must substantially improve it[78] within any thirty-month period after acquisition.

WHAT "SUBSTANTIAL IMPROVEMENT" MEANS

The rule is simple in principle: over a thirty-month period, you must increase the adjusted basis (excluding land value) of the property by at least 100 percent.[79] In practice, that means capital investments—major rcnovations, structural upgradcs, cxpansions—not just rcpairs or maintenance.

---

78. Treas. Reg. § 1.1400Z2(d)-1
79. IRC § 1400Z-2(d)(2)(D)(ii)

For rural OZ projects that use a Qualified Rural Opportunity Fund (QROF), the threshold is relaxed to 50 percent of basis, rather than 100 percent. That change was one of the deliberate tweaks in OZ 2.0 to make rural deals more practical.

TIMING IS EVERYTHING

Delays in permitting, construction, financing, or approvals can eat into your thirty-month window. Missing it means your property no longer qualifies as Qualified Opportunity Zone Property, which can jeopardize the QOF's compliance and trigger penalties.

WHAT COUNTS TOWARD IMPROVEMENT

Qualifying improvements must be capital expenditures: new construction, major systems (HVAC, plumbing, electrical), structural expansion, or full interior renovations. You can't use routine repairs, cosmetic fixes, or maintenance to satisfy this requirement. The expenditures must be capitalized into the property's basis.

ORIGINAL USE EXCEPTION AND VACANT PROPERTY

There is, however, a path around the thirty-month rule. If the property is brand new to the OZ (i.e., it hasn't been used there before) and is first placed in service after acquisition, you can satisfy the original use[80] standard and avoid the substantial improvement requirement entirely.

Also, a key exception exists for long-vacant property. If a building has been vacant for five years or more before acquisition, it can count as original use.[81] Similarly, a structure that never received a Temporary Certificate of Occupancy (TCO) may qualify, as it was never officially placed in service.

WHY IT MATTERS

This rule ensures OZ capital drives real physical transformation. It prevents passive investing—buying buildings and doing nothing—

---

80. Treas. Reg. § 1.1400Z2(d)-1(c)(7)

81. Treas. Reg.. § 1.1400Z2(d)-1(c)(7)(ii)(A)

and ensures that flows of capital are applied toward rehabilitation, upgrades, or redevelopment. Timing and capital planning are critical here. A deal that doesn't satisfy the substantial improvement test isn't just a missed tax opportunity—its eligibility may collapse.

Original Use vs. Substantial Improvement

To qualify a tangible property in an Opportunity Zone, you must satisfy one of two pathways: original use or substantial improvement. Choosing the right path is critical to your structuring and compliance.

ORIGINAL USE

A property meets the original use standard if it is *first placed in service within the Opportunity Zone after acquisition*. In other words, the asset must be new to that census tract—it hasn't been used there before.

If you qualify under original use, you avoid the obligation to double the basis (i.e., the thirty-month substantial improvement test). That means for new construction or brand-new assets in a zone, your capital investment doesn't need to flow into heavy renovations or upgrades within a fixed timeline.

The 90 Percent Asset Test for QOFs

Every QOF must pass a key compliance hurdle known as the 90 percent asset test. This rule ensures that a QOF actually channels its capital into Opportunity Zone property—not just parking it in cash or unrelated assets.

THE RULE

At least 90 percent of a QOF's assets must be invested in Qualified Opportunity Zone Property (QOZP). That includes two types of assets:

- equity investments in a Qualified Opportunity Zone Business (QOZB), which itself holds Qualified Opportunity Zone Business Property (QOZBP) and must pass a separate 70 percent test; and
- QOZBP which is held directly by the fund.

The 90 percent threshold is measured twice annually:

1. on the last day of the first six-month period of the fund's tax year, typically June 30; and
2. on the last day of the fund's tax year, typically December 31.

The average of those two tests must meet or exceed the 90 percent requirement.

WHY IT MATTERS

Failing the test has real consequences.

The IRS imposes monthly penalties on QOFs that fall short. And if noncompliance persists, the fund could lose its status entirely—putting investor tax benefits at risk.

HOW FUNDS STAY COMPLIANT

The vast majority of QOFs use a two-tier structure: the top-tier QOF raises capital from investors, then deploys it into a second-tier QOZB. The QOZB then owns the underlying assets, giving the fund more flexibility and time to meet asset and improvement requirements.

Understanding this structure—even as a limited partner (LP)—is vital. You're betting your tax benefits on the fund manager's operational discipline and timing precision.

Common Timing Pitfalls (OZ 2.0)

Opportunity Zones offer a uniquely powerful set of tax benefits, but those benefits are fragile. A single misstep in timing can erase the upside. Below are the most frequent timing traps I see.

MISSING THE 180-DAY REINVESTMENT WINDOW

This is by far the most common mistake. After you realize a gain, you generally have 180 days to get it into a QOF. Miss that window, and the gain is disqualified from OZ treatment—no deferral, no exclusion, no do-over. The IRS enforces this strictly.

MISINTERPRETING PASSTHROUGH ENTITY RULES

Gains from partnerships, S-corporations, or multi-member LLCs reported on K-1s have multiple possible start dates: sale date, entity tax year-end, or due date of return (without extension). The flexibility is useful, but it's also a trap if you pick the wrong start. In some cases, an investor might unintentionally fall into a dead period (when reinvestment is disqualified).[82]

SELLING BEFORE THE FIVE-YEAR MARK

If you sell your OZ investment before five years, your deferral is triggered early, and you lose the opportunity for the 10 percent or 30 percent basis step-up. Some investors misjudge liquidity needs or project timelines and find themselves boxed in.

SELLING BEFORE THE TEN-YEAR EXCLUSION

If your investment doesn't reach ten years, you lose the full exclusion on appreciation. All the growth is then taxed. Even one day early means no exclusion.

FAILING TO MEET THE THIRTY-MONTH SUBSTANTIAL IMPROVEMENT DEADLINE

When dealing with existing property, delays in construction, permits, supply chain issues, or capital allocation can cause you to miss the thirty-month improvement deadline. If the property fails to meet the improvement threshold, it might lose its OZ status—jeopardizing the entire fund.

MISSING ASSET TEST MEASUREMENT DATES

The 90 percent asset test is assessed twice a year.

If you don't balance your capital calls, acquisitions, and other capital deployments to meet those dates, you expose your fund to penalties—or worse, disqualification.

---

82. One example of a dead period: A passthrough gain realized on March 1. The taxpayer has an open window to invest from March 1 thru August 27, using the realization date as the start of the 180-day clock. But then, that taxpayer has a dead period from August 28 thru December 30. Another window opens up from December 31 thru September 10 of the following year, using either December 31 or March 15 of the following year as the start of the 180-day clock.

Why Timing Rules Exist

The timing rules in the Opportunity Zones statute aren't arbitrary—they're intentional. They reflect a deeper alignment between policy goals and investor incentives. In practice, these deadlines address two key tensions:

1. encouraging long-term capital, not short flips; and
2. ensuring capital is deployed quickly, not parked idle.

The five-year deferral, ten-year exclusion, and thirty-month improvement rule all push investors toward patience and persistence. At the same time, the 180-day window and semiannual asset tests require discipline, speed, and active management.

If you view the rules as mere hoops, you miss the point. They're the scaffolding of the program: designed so that OZ capital reaches communities in need, grounds itself in real projects, and remains committed over time.

In OZ investing, deadlines and clocks aren't nuisances; they're levers. If you understand the timing rules, you can design a deal that minimizes risk and maximizes return. Miss a date, and you could lose everything.

Timing affects the following:

- the entry date determines when your five-year deferral begins;
- the duration of your hold determines if you'll earn the full ten-year exclusion;
- the thirty-month clock for improvements dictates how you phase construction and capital deployment;[83] and
- the semiannual asset tests influence when to call capital, monetize assets, or close deals.

Think of timing as the architecture around which you build your investment.

---

83. The thirty-month substantial improvement period applies only to existing assets that are being improved. An asset that qualifies as original use need not adhere to this timeline.

You don't just pick a project and hope it fits. You structure it from the ground up to match the timing rules. That means working backward from exit, planning ahead for improvements, and coordinating with partners so that every milestone aligns.

Seasoned OZ sponsors treat timing as a competitive advantage. They build guardrails, buffers, and fallback options into their models. They don't assume things will run perfectly—but they do ensure compliance even when things go sideways. That's how they proactively protect the tax benefits up front through planning and structuring, rather than waiting until after problems occur and trying to salvage compliance retroactively.

If you can think in dates as easily as you think in dollars, you'll see places where small calendar tweaks (or gain-recognition delays) can change after-tax returns by tens of percentage points. Timing isn't a side constraint. In OZ investing, it's a core dimension of strategy.

Is OZ a Fit for You?

Now that you've seen how OZ advantages layer, and how timing rules protect or jeopardize them, the question becomes: Does this approach match your goals, strengths, and constraints?

OZ investing isn't for everyone. It rewards discipline, long horizons, compliance rigor, and operational bandwidth. If you prefer quick flips, maximum liquidity, or speculative plays in high-income neighborhoods, OZs will frustrate you more than help.

However, if you're an investor or sponsor who thinks in decades, who sees tax strategy as part of the investment thesis, who has the ability to commit capital and manage deadlines, that's where OZs shine. They can turn a cycle-agnostic hold into permanent, tax-free gains.

Also, Opportunity Zones pair especially well with high-gain events: sales of businesses, stocks, and real estate flips. If you have a capital gain that's sizable and taxable, rolling it into OZs can transform what would have gone to the IRS into patient, income-producing capital working in underserved zones.

Taxpayers with constant capital gains, even though smaller in magnitude, may also be attracted to OZ investing since it provides a long-term safety valve for tax deferral and long-term investing.

Of course, you still need due diligence: the underlying deal matters. A solid OZ structure won't salvage a bad location, weak fundamentals, or unfinished compliance planning. But layered onto a strong project, it can tilt the edge in your favor.

Now let's move from theory to real-world application.

CHAPTER FOUR

WHO SHOULD INVEST IN OPPORTUNITY ZONES?

THE OPPORTUNITY ZONE PROGRAM isn't for everyone.

The tax advantages are powerful, but they come with strings. This chapter is about filtering. It's designed to help you determine whether OZ investing actually fits your financial picture, your goals, and your risk tolerance.

By now, you've got the foundation. You understand what OZs are, how OZ 2.0 reformed the rules, and how the tax benefits work. Naturally, the next question becomes: *Should I invest in Opportunity Zones?*

The honest answer is that not everyone should.

In fact, for many investors, OZs aren't the right fit at all. The program requires a specific kind of capital, capital gains, and a specific kind of mindset: patient, long-term, and strategic. This isn't money you might need next year. It's capital that can afford to stay committed for a decade or more.

In this chapter, we'll walk through the investor profiles that stand to benefit the most and, just as importantly, the ones that don't. This isn't about pitching OZs to everyone. It's about helping you self-identify. If you see yourself in these profiles, you'll be well-positioned for the five-step OZ investing framework in the next chapter. If not, that's okay. There are plenty of other tax strategies out there that may fit your needs better.

Think of this chapter as a decision point. By the end, you should know whether Opportunity Zones belong in your portfolio—or whether they're best left on the shelf.

Taxpayer Profiles That Benefit Most

Opportunity Zones are especially attractive for high-net-worth individuals and families. Someone selling a $10 million business stands to benefit far more than someone with a $10,000 gain from a few shares of stock. The math scales fast, and so do the stakes.

Structure matters, too.

While individuals can invest directly, so can partnerships, trusts, and corporations. Partnerships, in particular, introduce a layer of strategy. Each partner can elect their own 180-day reinvestment window, opening the door to timing plays that enhance flexibility. No matter the entity type, the key is simple: you need eligible gains, and you need the willingness to commit.

Commitment is everything.

This isn't a program for short-term parking. To unlock the full benefits, you need to hold for ten years. That's when the magic happens: the complete elimination of capital gains tax on appreciation. There are interim benefits along the way, but the real upside is backloaded. That means the best-fit investors are those who can afford to be patient, those with capital that can stay planted for a decade or more.

This brings us to age and life stage. OZs are ideal for investors with long investment horizons. If you're still building wealth, or in the early stages of retirement, or a wealthy family with an inter-generational investment horizon, this may be a fit. But if you're in your twilight years and likely to need liquidity in five years or less, the program's incentives may not line up with your timeline.

So, who benefits most?

- Taxpayers with large, recent capital gains.
- Investors in higher tax brackets looking for strategic deferral and elimination.

- Those comfortable with long-term holds and illiquid positions.
- Entities, individuals, and families who can structure flexible timing around their reinvestment.

Opportunity Zones aren't for everyone. But for the right profile, they can be transformative: a tool for turning today's gains into tomorrow's tax-free growth.

Investment Goals and Liquidity Considerations

OZs align best with investors focused on long-term, tax-efficient growth. If your goal is to defer today's tax liability, keep more of your capital compounding, and exit in a decade with zero tax on appreciation, this framework offers a rare opportunity. But it's not without trade-offs.

One of the biggest trade-offs is liquidity.

Once your gains are reinvested into a Qualified Opportunity Fund (QOF), that money is effectively locked. It won't be available for day-to-day expenses, emergency spending, or short-term market plays. You're making a ten-year bet—not just on the investment, but on your ability to leave it untouched. If you foresee a need for access to those funds within a few years, OZs simply aren't the right vehicle.

That's why Opportunity Zone investments should never be your only strategy. They're not meant to replace core holdings or safety nets. They work best as a piece of a broader financial picture—paired with other, more liquid assets. Before allocating to an OZ fund, it's wise to ensure you have adequate reserves: cash savings, bonds, or other publicly traded securities that can cover short- and medium-term needs.

There's also the question of scale.

This program was designed to reward sizable gains. The tax incentives become most compelling when you're dealing with meaningful amounts—six figures, seven figures, or more. If you've just exited a business, sold a large real estate asset, or liquidated a substantial portfolio, the value proposition shifts. At that scale, the ability to compound capital tax-free for a decade can be transformational.

On the flip side, if your gain is small—say $10,000 from a few appreciated shares—the friction of illiquidity, fund fees, and investment risk could outweigh the benefit. OZs are not optimized for small gains or investors without other sources of accessible capital.

In short, OZs are a strategy for patient, strategic, and well-capitalized investors. It rewards those who are clear on their long-term goals and comfortable sacrificing flexibility today for greater tax efficiency tomorrow. For those who need near-term access to capital—or who are navigating gains too modest to justify the commitment—there may be better tools in the tax-planning toolbox.

Risk Tolerance and Sector Preference

Opportunity Zones are not low-risk investments.

That's an essential truth.

By their very nature, OZ projects often involve ground-up development, adaptive reuse, or the growth of early-stage businesses. These are ventures with moving parts: construction schedules, entitlement risk, market cycles, and operational complexity. They don't come with guarantees.

Real estate development, for example, carries a full stack of execution risk. From permitting delays and rising material costs to construction hiccups and shifting tenant demand, each stage introduces variables that can impact both timing and return. Investing in an OZ business—whether it's a manufacturing company, a healthcare startup, or a mission-driven local venture—brings its own set of challenges: leadership execution, scalability, market fit, and access to customers.

But that's the trade-off. Higher risk, higher reward.

The Opportunity Zone tax incentives are designed to compensate for that risk. If you succeed—if the project delivers—the upside is unmatched: long-term, tax-free growth on all post-investment appreciation. Remove the tax benefits, and many OZ deals look like traditional private equity or development plays: illiquid, longer-term, and built around the potential for outsized returns.

This is why sector preference matters.

Some investors naturally lean toward real estate. It's tangible. It's familiar. It comes with depreciation benefits and historically strong performance in inflationary environments. For these investors, OZs add a powerful tax wrapper to an asset class they already understand.

Others are drawn to operating businesses, especially those in growth sectors like tech, advanced manufacturing, or energy. These deals carry more volatility but also more potential for impact and exponential growth. In the right hands, an OZ business investment can generate returns that far exceed what's typical in real estate.

The key is alignment—with your risk profile, your portfolio, and your goals.

If you're primarily focused on capital preservation, liquidity, or low-volatility income, OZs may not be the right fit. But if you're comfortable with the risk-return dynamics of private equity or opportunistic real estate, and you're already comfortable allocating to alternative assets, OZs may be one of the most tax-efficient strategies available.

Accredited vs. Non-Accredited Investors

Most QOFs are built for accredited investors.

That's not a feature of the OZ statute itself; it's a function of securities law.[84] The majority of QOFs are structured as private offerings under Regulation D, which limits participation to individuals or entities that meet the accredited investor definition. In practice, that means the door is wide open for some, and much narrower for others.

Accreditation is determined by income, net worth, or professional credentials. For individuals, the standard thresholds are straightforward: $200,000 in annual income (or $300,000 with a spouse) for the past two years, or a net worth exceeding $1 million, excluding the primary residence. Certain financial professionals also qualify

84. Regulation D, 17 C.F.R. §§ 230.501–230.508.

automatically, including those holding Series 7, 65, or 82 licenses. Entities can qualify with $5 million in assets or if all equity owners are themselves accredited.[85]

For accredited investors, the landscape is robust.

You'll find a broad menu of professionally managed QOFs ranging from diversified real estate portfolios to targeted, single-asset deals and even sector-specific operating companies. These funds often offer institutional-grade management, detailed reporting, and built-in compliance infrastructure. In short, they make OZ investing turnkey.

For non-accredited investors, access is more limited.

That doesn't mean participation is impossible, but it does mean the path is less paved. Most private funds are off-limits, so alternative routes must be considered.

One option is to form a self-directed or captive QOF. For example, a business owner who sells appreciated property might reinvest the gain into a project they control—effectively creating their own fund. Another route is participating in a small, closely held fund designed for friends and family investors, though these structures come with legal complexity and higher execution risk.

These approaches require initiative. They demand legal guidance, compliance planning, and a high degree of investor sophistication. For newer or less experienced investors, the DIY route may introduce more friction than benefit.

The bottom line: Opportunity Zones favor accredited investors. If you meet the criteria, you'll find no shortage of professionally managed QOFs seeking capital. If not, the program is still accessible, but the path is steeper—and often best pursued by those with direct control over the projects they invest in.

---

85. "Accredited Investors," US Securities and Exchange Commission, updated August 13, 2025, https://www.sec.gov/resources-small-businesses/capital-raising-building-blocks/accredited-investors

Active vs. Passive Investor Roles

Opportunity Zones accommodate both active and passive investors, but the experience is fundamentally different.

Active investors take the driver's seat. They launch their own QOFs, source deals, oversee development or operations, and bear the responsibility for compliance. For developers, entrepreneurs, or business owners with projects in OZs, this route can be a natural fit. It offers control, customization, and the potential to capture both project-level profits and the full suite of OZ tax benefits.

But that control comes with real weight.

Running a fund means navigating complex legal structures, filing the right forms at the right times, ensuring that capital stays compliant, and managing risk across real assets or operating businesses. It's not just about investing—it's about operating. For those without prior experience in real estate, business growth, or fund management, the learning curve can be steep, even with professional legal counsel.

Passive investors, by contrast, contribute capital gains into professionally managed QOFs. From there, the sponsor handles everything: deal sourcing, underwriting, asset management, and regulatory compliance. This approach appeals to high-net-worth individuals, family offices, and those who want the benefits of OZ investing without the burden of direct oversight.

The trade-off is clear.

As a passive investor, you give up control, but you gain convenience, diversification, and access to teams with deep sector expertise. Instead of relying on your own involvement, you're betting on the sponsor's ability to execute, manage risk, and deliver returns.

Neither path is inherently better; it all comes down to fit.

If you're entrepreneurial, experienced, and motivated to build something from the ground up, the active approach gives you freedom and upside. But if your priority is tax-efficient growth with minimal distraction from your primary focus—whether that's running your business, managing your wealth, or simply preserving your time—the passive route offers a cleaner, simpler path.

Opportunity Zone investing can work either way. The question is: do you want to manage the vehicle or simply ride in it?

OZs for Real Estate Investors vs. Business Owners

OZs were designed with flexibility, but two groups stand out as natural beneficiaries:

- real estate investors
- business owners

Both can harness the program's tax advantages, but they do so through very different lenses, with distinct strategies, risks, and rewards.

For real estate investors, the OZ framework feels intuitive.

Many QOFs are built around development or redevelopment projects—acquiring land, constructing buildings, and/or undertaking substantial improvements to existing buildings.

These projects align cleanly with the OZ compliance structure, particularly the original use and substantial improvement rules. If you're already comfortable with permitting, entitlements, construction, and leasing, OZs simply add another layer of upside, particularly when paired with real estate's traditional tax benefits, such as depreciation and cost segregation.

In short, OZs amplify what developers already do well: build, improve, hold, and harvest gains.

For business owners, the path is different, but just as powerful.

Instead of investing in property, a business owner can qualify their company as a QOZB by locating operations in an OZ and meeting a set of IRS criteria around active trade or business requirements.[86] This creates an opportunity to raise equity capital from OZ investors, who in turn receive the same powerful tax treatment as they would from a real estate project.

This is a game-changer.

---

86. Refer to Treas. Reg. § 1.1400Z2(d)-1(d) for the IRS regulatory language on active trade or business requirements for a QOZB.

A high-growth company—especially one in manufacturing, technology, or healthcare—can tap OZ capital not just as financing, but as a competitive advantage. It creates alignment between investor return and community impact. And for the business owner, it opens the door to more favorable terms and mission-aligned capital.

The trade-offs are worth noting, though.

Real estate comes with construction risk, capital intensity, and market timing. But it also offers tangible assets, income predictability (once an asset is stabilized), and collateral. Business investments, by contrast, involve operational complexity—hiring, scaling, execution, and navigating competitive landscapes. But with that complexity comes the potential for outsized returns, especially if the business thrives.

The common thread is appreciation.

Whether you're developing mixed-use real estate or scaling a regional business, the program rewards long-term value creation. OZs don't pick winners—they reward builders. If your project or company can grow over time, and you're prepared to navigate the compliance structure, the upside is real.

Real estate or business. Bricks or ideas. Either path can work—if you play it smart and play it long.

When OZs Are Not the Right Fit

For all their advantages, Opportunity Zones are not a one-size-fits-all solution.

The program is purpose-built for a specific type of capital and a specific kind of investor. Recognizing where OZs don't fit is just as important as understanding where they do. Clear expectations are essential to making the right decision.

First and foremost, if you don't have capital gains, the incentive simply doesn't apply. Ordinary income, wages, savings, or other non-gain dollars are ineligible for the OZ tax benefits. Without a realized gain, there is no deferral, no reduction, and no excluded capital gains benefit to unlock. [87]

Second, Opportunity Zones are a poor fit for investors who need near-term liquidity. This is a long-hold strategy. If you know you'll need access to your capital in the next few years—for retirement, a major purchase, or emergency reserves—then tying it up in a ten-year vehicle is not just unwise; it could be financially damaging.

Third, the risk profile matters. OZ investments are not bond ladders or index funds. They involve construction, redevelopment, or early-stage operating businesses. These are projects that come with execution risk, regulatory complexity, and market exposure. If you have a low risk tolerance, or if the idea of delays, cost overruns, or startup volatility makes you uneasy, OZs are unlikely to align with your comfort zone.

Finally, compliance is non-negotiable.

This program runs on rules. QOFs and QOZBs must operate within a tightly defined regulatory framework, with deadlines, asset tests, and reporting requirements. If you're looking for a loophole or a casual workaround, this isn't it. OZs reward discipline, not shortcuts, and failure to comply can eliminate the very benefits the program promises.

In short, Opportunity Zones are not liquid. They are not low-risk. And they are not universally applicable. Knowing when to say no is just as valuable as knowing when to lean in.

---

87. A common question is whether after-tax, non-gain dollars can be invested to access at least the ten-year tax exclusion on appreciation of the OZ investment. The answer is no. While it may seem logical that such dollars could qualify for the long-term benefit, the law is clear: only capital gains are eligible for any Opportunity Zone tax advantages.

PART II

THE INVESTOR PLAYBOOK

CHAPTER FIVE

THE FIVE-STEP OPPORTUNITY ZONE INVESTING FRAMEWORK

NOW THAT WE'VE LAID THE GROUNDWORK for Opportunity Zones, we're going to shift from theory to execution.

OZ investing can be powerful, but it can also be complex. There are deadlines to meet, structures to understand, and deals to evaluate. Without a clear process, even the most motivated investor can get lost in the details.

That's where structure matters.

To invest successfully in Opportunity Zones, you need a framework: A repeatable roadmap that turns policy into strategy. One that simplifies the decision-making process and helps you move with clarity, confidence, and compliance.

Let's take a look at the five-step framework I use for successful OZ investing.

Step 1: Understand How the Program Can Grow Your Wealth

Before you evaluate deals or pick a fund, stop and ask the most important question: *what can this program actually do for me?*

Too many investors rush into Opportunity Zones without fully understanding the wealth-building mechanics. They get fixated on specific projects or sponsors and miss the larger point: OZs are not just about picking winners; they're about unlocking a unique tax structure that can dramatically accelerate long-term wealth creation.

UNLIMITED TAX-FREE GROWTH

This is the crown jewel of the OZ strategy.

If you hold your QOF investment for ten years or more, *all* of the appreciation—whether it doubles, triples, or explodes tenfold or more—can be realized with zero federal capital gains tax liability. There is no cap. No income limit. No gain ceiling.

The only limit is the strength of your investment and your patience.

This makes OZs uniquely positioned to support long-term growth strategies, whether through real estate development, operating businesses, or niche ventures in emerging markets. It's not just about sheltering tax; it's about building wealth that compounds tax-free.

A NON-CORRELATED PORTFOLIO DIVERSIFIER

OZ investments often move to a different rhythm than traditional asset classes. Real estate in emerging neighborhoods, local manufacturing startups, mission-aligned enterprises—these don't track the S&P 500. They operate on cycles shaped by geography, demand, and execution, not by short-term market volatility or earnings calls.

Allocating a portion of your capital gains to OZs doesn't just unlock tax benefits; it may also diversify your portfolio[88] into assets that often perform independently of public market volatility. That's a valuable hedge in any macro environment.

WHERE OZs FALL ON THE RISK-RETURN SPECTRUM

Let's be clear: this isn't a bond strategy.

---

88. This point about portfolio diversification is particularly true if your investment portfolio is allocated primarily among traditional assets (i.e., stocks and bonds). If you are already heavily invested in real estate, this point may not apply.

OZs live in the high-potential, high-risk segment of the investing universe. Projects often involve ground-up construction, value-add real estate, or early-stage operating businesses. These are inherently less predictable than buying a blue-chip stock or a Treasury bond.

But that risk is offset—significantly—by the tax benefits. The potential for tax-free appreciation changes the math. A good deal becomes a great one. An average return becomes exceptional. And for investors who understand and accept the risk, the upside is hard to ignore.

A WEALTH-BUILDING MINDSET

This is not a quick fix. It's not a loophole.

Opportunity Zones are designed to reward discipline. They're most effective when approached with a ten-year lens and a long-term philosophy. That's why your mindset matters. If you treat OZs as a serious part of your strategic wealth plan, rather than a year-end tax gimmick, you'll make better decisions at every stage of the journey.

From deal selection to due diligence to capital allocation, everything flows from this foundation.

Step 2: Generate an Eligible Gain

Every Opportunity Zone investment begins with the same starting point: a capital gain.

The rules around what qualifies are surprisingly broad. An eligible gain can come from the sale of publicly traded securities: stocks, bonds, mutual funds, and ETFs. It can come from selling investment real estate, whether a rental property, an apartment building, or even raw land. It can also come from a business exit, a partnership interest, or private equity. Gains from the sale of digital assets like Bitcoin and other cryptocurrencies are also eligible, as are gains from collectibles like art, classic cars, and even comic books, to name just a few examples.

If the IRS recognizes it as a capital gain,[89] there's a good chance it can be reinvested into a QOF.

Timing is everything, though.

Once the gain is realized, the clock starts. In most cases, you have 180 days to roll the gain into a QOF. Miss that window, and the opportunity closes. For most individuals, the countdown starts on the date of sale. But for passthrough entity gains—such as those reported on a Schedule K-1—or for installment sales and Section 1231 gains, the IRS allows certain elections that can delay the start of that 180-day clock. These options can create strategic flexibility, but the principle remains unchanged: the tax benefit only exists inside a window. And the window doesn't stay open long.

This step is foundational. Too often, investors get excited about the OZ incentive and start chasing deals before they've even identified the source of their eligible gain. That's a misstep. Everything flows from here. Without a gain, there is no deferral. No exclusion. No tax strategy to deploy.

This is the fuel that powers the entire engine.

For some investors, Step 2 begins naturally with the sale of a business, the liquidation of appreciated securities, or the closing of a real estate deal. For others, it may require deliberate action, such as harvesting gains from a portfolio in anticipation of making an OZ investment. Either way, once the gain is triggered, it sets everything else in motion.

Mark your calendar. Because from the moment the gain is realized, the countdown has begun.

Step 3: Pick Your OZ Investment Strategy

Once you've generated an eligible gain and are ready to deploy capital, the next decision is strategic: *how* do you want to participate in Opportunity Zones? This is where you choose your overall approach:

---

89. "Topic No. 409, Capital Gains and Losses," Internal Revenue Service, updated January 5, 2026, https://www.irs.gov/taxtopics/tc409

whether you want diversification, focused exposure, or complete control over the investment process.

There are three primary paths.

The first is investing as a limited partner in a professionally managed multi-asset fund. This is the most common route for passive investors. These funds pool capital across several projects—whether real estate developments, operating businesses, or a mix—providing built-in diversification. The upside is risk spreading and professional oversight. The fund sponsor handles deal sourcing, asset management, and compliance. You simply invest and monitor. The trade-off, of course, is limited control. You won't be picking individual projects or steering fund strategy.

The second option is investing as an LP in a professionally managed single-asset deal.

In this model, your capital goes into one project: an apartment development, a commercial building, a manufacturing facility, or a startup. You gain the ability to underwrite that specific opportunity, get comfortable with the sponsor, and invest in something you believe in. But with that focus comes concentration risk. If the project struggles, there's no portfolio effect to cushion the downside.[90]

Still, for investors who prefer deal-level clarity and sponsor alignment, this can be a strong fit.

The third path is starting your own Qualified Opportunity Fund. This gives investors the ability to create a self-directed QOF tailored to their own strategy and objectives. For active investors, operators, or developers, that may mean using the fund to manage their own capital, select their own deals, and oversee execution directly. This structure offers maximum flexibility—but also maximum responsibility—requiring the sponsor to manage fund formation, compliance testing, reporting, and project execution.

But not every self-directed QOF is fully hands-on. Some high-net-worth investors use a self-directed QOF as a personalized investment

---

90. Of course, one could achieve diversification to protect against single-asset downside risk by investing across multiple single-asset deals by multiple sponsors.

vehicle, then deploy that capital into professionally operated Qualified Opportunity Zone Businesses, co-invest alongside professional OZ sponsors, or otherwise outsource day-to-day execution while retaining control over capital allocation. In that sense, a self-directed QOF can be either an operating platform or simply a customized OZ investment wrapper. For experienced professionals and sophisticated investors, this can be a powerful structure. For others, it may introduce more complexity than value.

Each approach comes with clear trade-offs. Multi-asset funds offer diversification and ease, but little control. Single-asset deals offer sharper focus, but more risk. A self-directed fund offers complete control *and* complete responsibility. The right choice depends on your investing style, your experience, and how involved you want to be.

Passive or active? Diversified or concentrated? Outsourced or self-managed?[91]

Once you've selected your strategy, you can then layer in sector preferences. Some investors gravitate toward real estate—residential, mixed-use, industrial, etc.—because it's tangible and familiar. Others may be drawn to operating businesses, or niche categories like infrastructure, energy, or tech. All of these can qualify under the OZ rules when structured properly. But each comes with its own risk profile, timelines, and underwriting nuances.

Step 4: Pick the Specific Investments

Once you've chosen your overall strategy, the next step is to identify the actual investments.

This is where theory meets reality. Whether you're evaluating a multi-asset fund, a single-asset project, or a deal inside your own QOF, the focus now shifts to specific opportunities and the due diligence that comes with them.

At this stage, it's not about the program. It's about the project.

---

91. These strategies aren't mutually exclusive. With enough gains, an investor could choose to allocate across two or all three of these strategies.

You're no longer asking, *Should I invest in Opportunity Zones?* You're asking, *Should I invest in this specific deal or investment portfolio, with this specific sponsor, in this specific location?*

There are several core factors to evaluate. Start with the sponsor. Who's running the project? Do they have a proven track record of executing deals of similar size and complexity? What's their history with OZ compliance, development timelines, and investor communication?

In private market investing, the sponsor is often as important as the asset itself.

Next, assess the location. Not all Opportunity Zones are equal. Some are in transitional neighborhoods on the verge of growth. Others may face long-term economic headwinds. Look at local demographics, job growth, infrastructure plans, and market fundamentals. The right location can make or break the return profile.

Then, understand the project type. Is it ground-up construction? A redevelopment of an existing asset? An investment in an operating business? Each type comes with a different risk profile, timeline, and potential reward. Your comfort with those variables should match your investment goals.

Finally, review the deal structure. What are the fees? What's the profit split? Is the sponsor co-investing alongside you, or just managing other people's money? What happens in a downside scenario? How transparent is the reporting? These are the mechanics that determine whether your capital is protected and how you participate in the upside.

To help you evaluate these aspects with discipline, this book includes two practical tools in the Appendices. The first is the OZ Investor Readiness Checklist. This self-assessment helps you confirm that you're prepared to commit capital for a decade or more. It prompts the questions too many investors skip: Am I financially prepared? Have I reviewed the tax implications with my CPA? Am I clear on the risks?

The second is the OZ Investment Due Diligence Questionnaire. This tool helps you vet the investment itself. It outlines the questions you should be asking every sponsor before you write a check: What's the minimum investment? What's the pipeline? How diversified is the fund? What are the exit options? Does the sponsor have skin in the game?

Using these tools ensures that you don't just respond to slick pitch decks or glossy brochures. You move from reacting to evaluating. You apply a consistent process that filters for quality and fits your strategy.

You also don't have to go it alone. We offer many opportunities to connect investors with OZ investments: our investment marketplace at OpportunityZones.com, our OZ Pitch Day events, and within our mastermind community, OZ Insiders. Whether you find deals through those platforms or elsewhere, the same rule applies: do the work before you wire the funds.

Step 5: Move the Money and Prep Your Tax Return

This is where strategy becomes reality. By now, you've chosen your investment approach, completed your due diligence, and selected a specific opportunity. Step 5 is about execution: formally funding the deal and documenting your participation in the program with the IRS.

It starts with moving the capital. When you wire your eligible gain into a Qualified Opportunity Fund (QOF), you're not just transferring money; you're making a tax election. The moment those funds land inside the QOF, you are signaling your intent to participate in the OZ program. The sponsor will provide subscription documents and an investor questionnaire that must be completed before your capital is accepted.

These aren't optional formalities; they are part of the securities law and OZ compliance record.

Think of this step in terms of a timeline:

- day 1: you realize a capital gain from the sale of an appreciated asset.

- by day 180: you reinvest that gain into a QOF. If you miss this window, the tax benefit is lost.
- by April 15 (or October 15, if extended) of the year after realizing your gain: you file IRS Form 8997[92] with your tax return to report the investment and make the deferral official.

These three milestones form the backbone of OZ compliance. If you hit them, your investment qualifies. If you miss them, even a good deal won't deliver the intended tax benefits.

Beyond the timeline, paperwork is critical. This is where many investors underestimate what's required. When you subscribe to a QOF, you'll receive a standard set of documents. These typically include:

- a subscription agreement, which formalizes your investment amount and admits you into the fund as a limited partner or member;
- an investor questionnaire, which is used to verify your accreditation status and comply with Know Your Customer and Anti-Money Laundering rules;
- an operating agreement or limited partnership agreement, which outlines management structure, profit splits, voting rights, reporting cadence, and sponsor responsibilities;
- additional exhibit acknowledgments, which disclose fees, potential conflicts of interest, and project-specific risks; and
- wiring instructions, which tell you how to move the money from your account into the QOF.

These documents create the official paper trail. They prove your capital was invested correctly and within the required timeframe.

On your side, the most important filing is IRS Form 8997, which must be submitted with your tax return in the year of your investment

92. "Form 8997: Initial and Annual Statement of Qualified Opportunity Fund (QOF) Investments," Internal Revenue Service, updated August 2, 2025, https://www.irs.gov/forms-pubs/about-form-8997

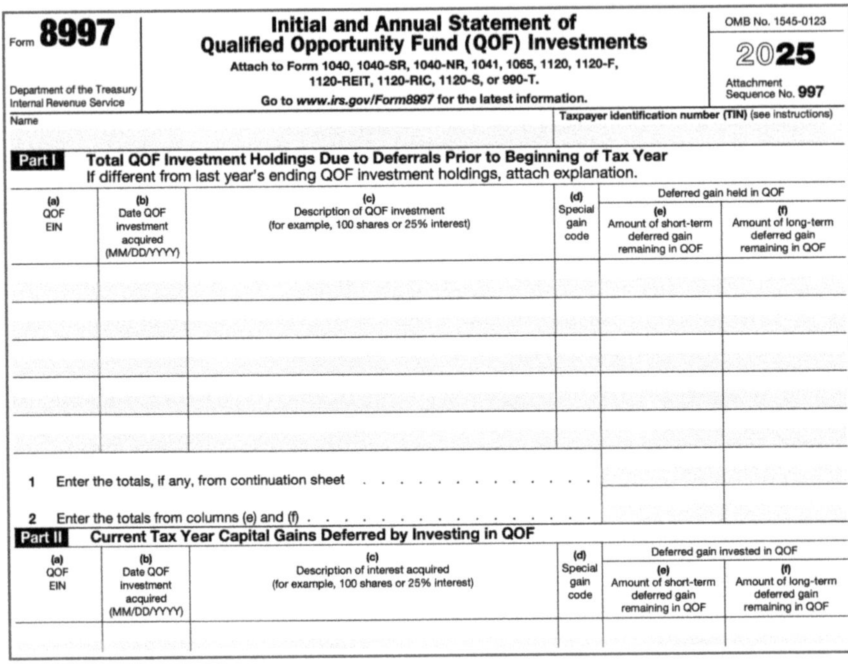

Form **8997** | **Initial and Annual Statement of Qualified Opportunity Fund (QOF) Investments** | OMB No. 1545-0123 **2025**

Department of the Treasury Internal Revenue Service

Attach to Form 1040, 1040-SR, 1040-NR, 1041, 1065, 1120, 1120-F, 1120-REIT, 1120-RIC, 1120-S, or 990-T.

Go to *www.irs.gov/Form8997* for the latest information.

Attachment Sequence No. **997**

Name | **Taxpayer identification number (TIN)** (see instructions)

Part I **Total QOF Investment Holdings Due to Deferrals Prior to Beginning of Tax Year**
If different from last year's ending QOF investment holdings, attach explanation.

(a) QOF EIN	(b) Date QOF investment acquired (MM/DD/YYYY)	(c) Description of QOF investment (for example, 100 shares or 25% interest)	(d) Special gain code	Deferred gain held in QOF: (e) Amount of short-term deferred gain remaining in QOF	(f) Amount of long-term deferred gain remaining in QOF

1 Enter the totals, if any, from continuation sheet . . . .

2 Enter the totals from columns (e) and (f) . . . .

Part II **Current Tax Year Capital Gains Deferred by Investing in QOF**

(a) QOF EIN	(b) Date QOF investment acquired (MM/DD/YYYY)	(c) Description of interest acquired (for example, 100 shares or 25% interest)	(d) Special gain code	Deferred gain invested in QOF: (e) Amount of short-term deferred gain remaining in QOF	(f) Amount of long-term deferred gain remaining in QOF

IRS Form 8997 is filed annually by investors who defer gains into one or more Qualified Opportunity Funds.

and every year thereafter, for as long as you hold the investment. This form records your election to defer the gain and identifies the specific QOF where you invested. If this form is missing or inaccurate, you risk losing the entire tax benefit, even if the investment itself was otherwise compliant.

Meanwhile, your fund sponsor will have their own reporting obligations to the IRS. But as the investor, your job is to keep everything organized and work closely with your tax professional. OZ investing is a long game, and your compliance trail needs to last a decade or longer.

Step 5 is also where professional guidance becomes essential. Your CPA should be looped in early in the process, but especially here, during funding and tax preparation.

Case Study: Walking Through the Framework on a Sample Deal

To bring the five-step Opportunity Zone investing framework to life, let's walk through a practical example from start to finish.

STEP 1: UNDERSTAND HOW THE PROGRAM CAN GROW WEALTH

Tom is a high-net-worth investor who just realized a $1 million capital gain. Before making any moves, he steps back to study the Opportunity Zone incentive. He learns how the program allows him to defer that gain, potentially reduce the amount he'll owe, and eliminate tax on all future appreciation, so long as he holds the OZ investment for ten years or more. The structure makes sense. The tax benefits are compelling. He begins to view OZs not just as a tax play, but as a long-term wealth-building strategy.

STEP 2: GENERATE AN ELIGIBLE GAIN

Tom's $1 million gain comes from the sale of appreciated stock.

That sale starts the 180-day countdown. He now has a fixed window to reinvest the gain into a QOF.

If he misses that window, the tax benefit disappears.

STEP 3: PICK AN INVESTMENT STRATEGY

Tom considers his options.

He could launch his own QOF and operate deals directly. He could invest in a single-asset project and underwrite one opportunity in depth. But he ultimately chooses to invest passively in a professionally managed multi-asset fund.

This gives him broad diversification and shifts the burden of management, reporting, and compliance to the sponsor.

STEP 4: PICK THE SPECIFIC INVESTMENTS

Tom shortlists several funds. Then he applies the tools from this book.

First, he uses the Investor Readiness Checklist to confirm he's financially and mentally prepared to lock up this capital for ten years or more. He loops in his CPA to ensure the tax implications are fully understood.

Then, he works through the Due Diligence Questionnaire, asking each fund about their track record, project pipeline, fees, co-investment, and exit strategy.

With that framework in hand, he selects one or more funds aligned with his long-term goals—led by a sponsor with a strong operating history and experience across OZ-compliant projects.

STEP 5: MOVE THE MONEY AND PREP THE TAX RETURN

Tom completes the subscription documents and wires his $1 million gain into the QOF(s) before the 180-day deadline. He then coordinates with his tax advisor to ensure Form 8997 is properly filed with his return for that tax year and each tax year thereafter as long as he is invested in at least one QOF.

With those steps complete, Tom is officially an Opportunity Zone investor.

THE OUTCOME

By investing within the 180-day window, Tom locks in the deferral of his $1 million capital gain. That tax bill is no longer due this year; it's pushed five years into the future. Depending on the zone type and his holding period, he may also qualify for a reduction in the recognized gain when that bill eventually comes due.

Ten years later, Tom's investment has grown to $2.5 million, and because he met the ten-year requirement, the $1.5 million in appreciation is completely excluded from federal capital gains tax. But Tom doesn't have to sell. He can continue holding and allow the investment to keep compounding tax-free for up to thirty years.

By year thirty, the investment is worth $5 million. Tom elects to step up the basis to fair market value. The entire $4 million in appreciation is excluded from tax. There's no federal capital gains liability. No depreciation recapture. No exit tax.

This is what sets Opportunity Zones apart. The incentive doesn't just defer the tax bill for a few years. It creates the legal and structural conditions for long-term, tax-free compounding—potentially over multiple decades. It's a path to generational wealth, and it starts with a simple, five-step framework.

Tom followed it. You can, too.

CHAPTER SIX

NAVIGATING OZ SECTORS AND REQUIREMENTS

NOW IT'S TIME TO SHIFT OUR FOCUS away from process and toward the investment landscape itself.

OZs are intentionally broad. They were designed to accommodate a wide range of asset types—from housing and commercial real estate to technology startups, healthcare companies, and even infrastructure projects—and this flexibility is one of the program's greatest strengths. It gives investors the freedom to match the tax benefits to their own investment thesis.

But that same flexibility can be a challenge.

With so many potential use cases, it's easy to get stuck in analysis paralysis—evaluating dozens of unrelated projects, comparing apples to oranges, and struggling to define a clear strategy. That's why it's so important to understand the core sectors where OZ capital tends to flow—and how each aligns with different investor goals, risk profiles, and timelines.

In this chapter, we'll explore the three major lanes for Opportunity Zone capital: real estate, operating businesses, and infrastructure and special-use projects.

Real Estate in OZs

Real estate has been the dominant sector in Opportunity Zones since day one.[93] It's a natural fit—tangible, familiar, and structurally aligned with the program's core requirements.

What makes it so effective is how seamlessly OZ rules map onto traditional development activity. The "original use" and "substantial improvement" tests, which can be challenging in other asset classes, are almost tailor-made for ground-up construction and major rehab projects. A vacant lot turned into housing? Compliant. An aging warehouse converted into a modern logistics hub? Also compliant.

This flexibility has drawn a wide mix of investors.

Some came with deep real estate experience: developers, family offices, certain high-net-worth investors. But many others were new to real estate altogether. The draw wasn't just the tax benefit. It was the way Opportunity Zones made development more accessible, often through structured, sponsor-led funds that handled compliance and execution.

Among real estate subsectors, multifamily housing has led the way, and with good reason. Many OZ tracts face acute housing shortages. Demographic trends support sustained rental demand, particularly for workforce and affordable housing. OZ capital has helped bridge the financing gap for developers building where the need is greatest.

Industrial real estate is another rising star. The explosion of e-commerce, the reshoring of manufacturing, and the demand for last-mile logistics space have pushed warehouses and distribution centers to the forefront. Opportunity Zones, often located in underutilized or transitional areas, are ideally positioned for this type of growth.

---

93. According to a May 2024 report by the Joint Committee on Taxation, 63 percent of QOF investments are in real estate, and another 16 percent are in related sectors like construction, finance, and insurance. The staff of the Joint Committee on Taxation, "Description of Qualified Opportunity Zone Tax Provisions and Analysis Of 2019-2022 Tax Return Data Related to Investments in Qualified Opportunity Zones," May 2024, https://www.jct.gov/getattachment/ea5be73e-1edd-441e-be31-eefd6b649e41/Opportunity-Zones-Tax-Provisions-Report-May-2024.pdf

Hospitality plays a smaller role. Hotels and resorts can pencil out well in certain OZs, particularly those near tourism hubs or growing business corridors, but they carry a higher risk. These projects are highly sensitive to travel cycles and macroeconomic conditions, which makes underwriting more volatile and investor appetite more selective.

Then there are mixed-use projects: ambitious, catalytic developments that combine residential, retail, office, and public spaces. When done right, they can transform entire neighborhoods. But they require more capital, longer timelines, and deeper coordination with municipalities and community stakeholders.

Then there's self-storage, single-family rentals (SFR), build-to-rent (BTR), retail, and more. Opportunity Zone real estate spans a wide range of property types, but regardless of strategy, compliance is key.

To qualify, a real estate project must either establish "original use" by developing on vacant land or meet the "substantial improvement" threshold by doubling the value of an existing building (excluding land) within a thirty-month period. Ground-up construction often tends to be the cleanest fit, both operationally and from a compliance standpoint.

Opportunity Zones didn't invent real estate investing. But they did supercharge it, especially for projects in places that might have struggled to attract private capital on their own.

And while real estate will likely remain the dominant use case for OZs, it's not the only one. Far from it. There's an entire class of operating businesses that can deliver even greater upside, and align just as well with the policy's original intent.

That's where we turn next.

Operating Businesses in OZs

While real estate has taken center stage in Opportunity Zone investing, the program was never meant to be just about buildings. From the outset, the policy was designed to do more than reshape skylines. It was built to spark entrepreneurship, generate jobs, and fuel long-term economic growth in underserved communities.

And that's where operating businesses come in.

A Qualified Opportunity Zone Business (QOZB) can take many forms. Manufacturing is one of the most straightforward. A factory, assembly plant, or fabrication facility located inside an OZ meets the program's geographic and asset-use tests while serving as a durable job creator for the local economy.

But manufacturing is just the beginning.

Technology companies are another powerful use case. Startups can launch in an OZ, and existing firms can relocate operations into qualifying tracts. Either path creates eligibility and opens the door to tax-advantaged capital that might not otherwise be available. For entrepreneurs, it's not just about tax treatment. It's about tapping into a new pool of growth capital and building in markets where early-stage innovation is often underfunded.

Service-based businesses also qualify. From healthcare providers and trade schools to consulting firms and logistics operators, any company conducting active business within a zone, and meeting the statutory thresholds, can participate. These types of businesses often have the most direct community impact, as they deliver essential services where they're needed most.

Compliance is critical here.

Unlike real estate, which benefits from clearer statutory alignment, operating businesses must meet multiple tests. At least 70 percent of their tangible property must be located in the zone. At least 50 percent of their gross income must come from the active conduct of business in the zone.[94] And they must avoid prohibited activities—golf courses, country clubs, massage parlors, hot tub facilities, tanning facilities, racetracks, or other facilities used for gambling, and liquor stores are explicitly excluded from OZ cligibility.[95]

The potential upside, however, is significant.

Whereas most real estate investments target modest, stable

---

94. There are four tests for determining 50 percent of gross income, which are detailed in Chapter 12.

95. This list of "sin businesses" is drawn from IRC § 144(c)(6)(B).

returns—perhaps a 2x to 3x equity multiple—operating businesses offer the possibility of exponential growth. A successful manufacturing plant might anchor hundreds of jobs. A breakout software company might deliver 10x or even 100x returns. For investors with the right risk appetite, that growth can translate into an extraordinary tax-free upside.

But the risks are real. Businesses, especially early-stage ones, can fail. Even seasoned operators face market shifts, regulatory headwinds, and execution challenges. There are fewer tangible assets to fall back on, and more operational variables to manage.

Still, for investors aligned with the core intent of the OZ program, operating businesses may represent the purest opportunity. They don't just defer taxes or shelter gains—they create engines of growth in the places that need them most.

And that's the heart of what Opportunity Zones were designed to do.

Infrastructure and Special-Use Projects

Not every Opportunity Zone investment fits neatly into the category of real estate or operating businesses. There's a third lane, one that blends physical development with public utility: infrastructure and special-use projects.

These are often large, capital-intensive initiatives with the potential to anchor regional growth and align with national priorities. Think energy, defense manufacturing, logistics, broadband, healthcare, education, and beyond.

Some of the clearest examples include energy production, such as oil and gas projects and solar projects. These energy assets not only serve the long-term shift toward more domestic energy production, but they also frequently pair with other incentives in the tax code. When layered with OZ equity, the financing stack can become a powerful tool for driving both returns and impact.

Data centers and telecom infrastructure also fit into this space. These projects expand digital capacity and bring high-speed connectivity to regions that have historically been underserved. In an increasingly digital economy, connectivity is not just a convenience; it's foundational. OZ capital can help bring that foundation to communities left behind by previous waves of investment.

Last-mile logistics centers add to the mix. These projects support regional commerce, strengthen supply chains, and attract adjacent industrial development. They can serve as economic engines for entire zones.

Shipbuilding and maritime manufacturing are also emerging as specialized Opportunity Zone use cases. In certain coastal markets, OZ capital is being deployed to expand domestic shipbuilding and naval supply-chain capacity, aligning private investment with national industrial and defense priorities.[96] Related initiatives such as Maritime Prosperity Zones may further strengthen the long-term policy tailwinds behind these strategically important projects.

Then there are sector-specific facilities like healthcare clinics, senior housing, and student residences. Each of these meets an essential need, often in communities where access is limited. They may not always grab headlines, but their social utility and long-term demand profiles make them attractive to both mission-driven and yield-focused investors.

But the appeal comes with complexity.

Unlike traditional real estate deals, these projects often involve multi-agency regulatory reviews, extended planning timelines, and intricate financing structures. Success may require combining OZ equity with local incentives, municipal bonds, or federal infrastructure grants. Zoning, permitting, and environmental approvals all add layers of challenge and delay.

---

96. CapZone Impact Investments announced in 2024 that it had deployed Opportunity Zone capital into a shipyard expansion project in Mobile, AL, aimed at increasing US nuclear submarine production capacity for the US Navy, highlighting the emerging use of OZ equity in strategic domestic manufacturing and defense-related infrastructure. "U.S. Navy Taps Opportunity Zone Fund To Expand Submarine Building Capacity," OpportunityZones.com, September 24, 2024, https://opportunityzones.com/2024/09/u-s-navy-taps-opportunity-zone-fund-to-expand-submarine-building-capacity/

This is not beginner territory. But for experienced sponsors and investors with the patience and expertise to navigate the hurdles, infrastructure and special-use projects can deliver powerful results. They can serve as anchors—stabilizing communities, attracting follow-on capital, and setting the stage for multi-decade growth.

In short, these projects don't just fit inside Opportunity Zones.

They *build* them.

Single-Asset QOFs

One of the first decisions that sponsors and investors face in OZs is whether to structure a Qualified Opportunity Fund (QOF) around a single project or to pool multiple assets. A single-asset QOF is exactly what it sounds like: a fund created to own one deal—one property, one business, one opportunity.

The appeal lies in its simplicity. Investors know precisely what they're buying into. The vision can be clearly articulated, the pro forma transparent, and the entire capital stack focused on a single venture. When a sponsor has high conviction—whether in a development site, an operating business, or an infrastructure play—a single-asset fund creates tight alignment.

Everyone's upside (and downside) is tied to the same outcome.

That clarity, however, comes with concentration risk. There's no diversification; no portfolio to smooth out winners and losers. If the project performs, returns can be outstanding. If it misses, there's no buffer. Liquidity is another constraint. Because the fund revolves around a single exit, distributions are typically dependent on one event, which can complicate timing and limit investor flexibility.

Single-asset QOFs tend to be best suited for experienced operators who have a specific deal in hand and the expertise to execute it. These sponsors often bring unique access to a site or strategy they know intimately. Investors who want targeted exposure to that particular project, rather than allocating capital to a blind pool, may also find this model attractive.

This structure has been common in the Opportunity Zone space. Many OZ sponsors launch single-asset QOFs to pursue a clear, one-off opportunity. It remains a valid approach, but one that requires investors to be comfortable with the risk profile, execution reliance, and absence of diversification.

Multi-Asset QOFs

At the opposite end of the spectrum from single-project vehicles are multi-asset QOFs.

These funds pool capital and invest across multiple projects, businesses, or both—offering diversification across sectors, geography, or sometimes, both.

- Sector diversification might mean one fund holds multifamily housing, industrial warehouses, and perhaps even an operating business. Different asset types behave differently across market cycles. Hospitality might slump during a downturn, while workforce housing holds steady. Industrial demand could surge from e-commerce, even if local retail lags. Mixing asset classes helps cushion against concentrated risk.
- Geographic diversification adds another layer of protection. A fund could span fast-growing Sun Belt cities, legacy Midwest manufacturing corridors, and coastal innovation hubs. Local economies respond to different forces, some demographic, others regulatory or political. By spreading exposure, the fund is less likely to be derailed by any single region's hiccup.

Some funds do both—diversifying across different asset classes and locations. This can result in a portfolio where no single project, geography, or sector carries too much weight. For investors, that means a smoother ride, steadier performance, and less anxiety about any one deal going sideways.

But diversification isn't just about spreading risk. It also creates exit flexibility. After the ten-year hold, a multi-asset QOF doesn't need to liquidate all at once. The sponsor can exit some deals, refinance others, or hold promising assets longer. That optionality can help match investor liquidity needs with market timing.

Of course, complexity comes with the territory. Managing a multi-asset QOF requires coordinating compliance across multiple entities, tracking different construction or business timelines, and communicating with investors about a moving target. Fees may be higher. And in a blind pool, investors must place real trust in the sponsor's vision and execution.

Still, for many investors, the benefits are worth it.

Multi-asset funds offer hands-off access to professional management and a built-in risk spread. They align well with investors who prefer diversified exposure to Opportunity Zones without betting the farm on a single project.

When managed by an experienced sponsor with a track record, a multi-asset QOF can deliver on what Opportunity Zones were meant to do—provide long-term, tax-advantaged growth while building real economic value in underserved communities.

Captive QOFs

These are self-directed vehicles formed by high-net-worth individuals or family offices to manage their own capital gains.[97] Captive QOFs don't raise outside money. Their sole purpose is to wrap a specific investment, or set of investments, in an OZ-compliant structure, allowing the investor to control deployment while capturing the tax benefits.

They're especially useful for investors who want to fund their own projects, back related businesses, or make highly customized investments without giving up control.

97. "The Two Ways To Invest In Opportunity Zones (Active vs Passive)", OpportunityZones.com, December 31, 2025, https://opportunityzones.com/guide/ways-to-invest/ describes the "captive or self-funded QOF" strategy.

The takeaway is simple: there's no one-size-fits-all model.

Single-asset QOFs offer clarity and focus. Multi-asset funds provide diversification and scale. Captive QOFs maximize control and customization.

Each has its place.

As an investor, it's not enough to understand the project. You also need to understand how the fund is structured, because that structure will shape everything from compliance risk to reporting timelines to how and when you get paid.

Structure isn't just a legal formality. It's part of the strategy.

Sector-Specific Compliance Requirements

Each sector in the Opportunity Zone universe comes with its own compliance playbook, but the overarching framework remains the same: reinvest capital gains into a QOF, deploy into qualifying assets, hold for at least ten years. . . but the rules shift based on the kind of asset you're investing in.

In real estate, the two big tests are original use and substantial improvement.

New construction generally qualifies under original use, since the property hasn't been placed in service before. For existing structures, however, the fund must substantially improve the asset, doubling its basis (excluding land value) within a thirty-month period.

Operating businesses face an entirely different compliance framework. To qualify as a QOZB, at least 70 percent of the company's tangible property must be located in an Opportunity Zone. Additionally, at least 50 percent of its gross income must come from actively conducting business within the zone. And no more than 5 percent of its assets can be non-qualified financial property, like cash equivalents or passive investments.

These rules are designed to ensure OZ capital fuels real economic activity on the ground, not just idle balance sheets. For founders and sponsors, staying compliant means tracking where the business operates, how its income is earned, and where its assets sit, year after year.

Special-use projects—like solar farms, affordable housing, or healthcare facilities—often layer OZ equity with other public or private incentives. That can be powerful but also complicated. A renewable energy project might also depend on federal tax credits, state subsidies, or utility contracts. An affordable housing development could involve HUD financing and low-income housing tax credits (LIHTCs). Each of these programs has its own reporting schedules, eligibility rules, and oversight regimes, and they all have to be synchronized with Opportunity Zone requirements.

That means more structuring complexity and a higher need for specialized advisors who can manage multiple systems in parallel.

Aligning Sector Choice with Investor Goals

By now, it should be clear: Opportunity Zones are not a one-size-fits-all strategy. The sector you choose should align directly with your investment objectives, time horizon, and appetite for risk.

Investors prioritizing stability often gravitate toward multifamily housing or diversified real estate funds. These projects benefit from consistent demand, tangible assets, and well-understood underwriting. Some real estate may also offer a natural hedge against inflation, which makes it appealing for those seeking reliable, long-term exposure with the potential for steady cash flow.

Those with a higher risk tolerance might be drawn to operating businesses. Startups and private enterprises carry more uncertainty, but they also offer a greater upside. Investing in a manufacturing plant, a regional logistics company, or a tech-enabled service provider could yield returns far above what an apartment development project might deliver. For the right investor, there's added satisfaction in funding job creation and revitalizing local economies, which is the very heart of the OZ program's policy intent.

Infrastructure and special-use projects often attract investors looking to pair long-term impact with long-hold capital. These may not offer immediate liquidity, but they create backbone assets—solar fields, fiber networks, healthcare hubs—that can shape entire regions for decades. For some, the appeal lies in aligning capital with national priorities like domestic energy production, defense manufacturing, or housing.

Time horizon matters, too.

Real estate might take years to build and stabilize, but once operational, it can offer predictable income. Operating businesses may spin up revenue faster but are more vulnerable to market and execution risk. Infrastructure typically requires longer entitlement and planning periods, but the outcome can be deeply durable value.

Portfolio fit is another factor.

An investor heavily weighted in real estate might use OZs to branch into operating businesses. A growth-focused investor may view OZs as a chance to pursue higher-upside ventures that are enhanced by the tax treatment.

Meanwhile, some investors may prefer multi-asset funds that blend sectors and geographies, with professional managers handling compliance behind the scenes.

Ultimately, the sector decision shouldn't be based on what's trending. It should be driven by what *you* need. Do you want stability or growth? Passive exposure or hands-on involvement? Cash flow or long-term capital appreciation?

Choosing the right sector means matching the tool to the task, and making sure the OZ incentive amplifies your broader wealth-building strategy, not just your tax planning.

CHAPTER SEVEN

HOW OZ FUNDS ARE STRUCTURED

NOW IT'S TIME TO zoom in on the investment vehicle at the center of all OZ endeavors: the Qualified Opportunity Fund (QOF). To truly understand how a QOF works and why its structure matters, we need to step back and look at the broader private fund universe.

What Is a Private Fund?

Before diving into the specifics of QOFs, it helps to step back and understand the broader category they belong to: private funds.[98]

At its core, a private fund is simply a pooled investment vehicle. Multiple investors contribute capital into a single entity, which is then managed by a sponsor who makes the investment decisions. If you've ever invested in a mutual fund or exchange-traded fund, the basic concept is familiar: a group of investors pools money together, and a professional manager allocates that money into a portfolio of publicly traded stocks and/or bonds.

98. There are, in fact, two publicly traded Qualified Opportunity Funds: Belpointe REIT (ticker symbol OZ on NYSE American) and Park View OZ REIT (ticker symbol PVOZ on the OTC Pink Market). But these are the only two exceptions. All other Qualified Opportunity Funds are privately offered.

The key difference is that private funds operate outside the public markets. They are not sold on an exchange, they are not registered with the Securities and Exchange Commission (SEC) like mutual funds and ETFs, and they are not available to the general public.

Instead, a private fund is generally offered under a Regulation D SEC exemption and sold almost exclusively to accredited investors.[99] (SEC exemptions are covered in more detail in Part III of this book.) This means they are designed for investors with a certain level of income, net worth, or professional sophistication—people presumed to be able to bear the risks of private investments. Because of this exemption, private funds avoid many of the regulatory burdens that come with public offerings. Nevertheless, they are still subject to securities laws and investor protection rules.

Structurally, most private funds are organized as limited partnerships or limited liability companies. These formats provide two essential advantages.

First, they shield a fund's passive investors from personal liability: investors cannot lose more than the amount they have invested. Second, they give the fund manager flexibility in allocating profits and losses.

Unlike public companies, where distributions follow rigid share ownership rules, private funds can be structured with preferred returns, profit splits, and incentive arrangements that reward the manager only after investors achieve a certain return.

A simple example helps bring this down to earth.

Imagine a developer wants to build a $20 million apartment complex in a growing city. It secures a construction loan for $12 million

---

99. There are many types of SEC exemptions, including Reg A, Reg A+, Reg CF, and Reg D. Some of the exemptions even allow for non-accredited investors to participate. But in practice, the vast majority of Qualified Opportunity Funds are offered under Reg D, using either Rule 506(b) or Rule 506(c). While funds offered under Rule 506(b) of Reg D allow for up to thirty-five non-accredited investors to participate, in practice very few fund managers employing Rule 506(b) for their offerings permit non-accredited investors to participate anyway.

from a bank, which means $8 million of equity is still needed. Instead of funding all $8 million itself, the developer creates a private fund. It invites ten investors to each contribute $800,000, and those investors become limited partners in the fund. The developer, acting as the fund's manager, oversees the project: acquiring the land, managing construction, leasing up the units, and eventually selling the building. The investors share in the profits according to the fund's operating agreement, while the developer may also receive additional upside if the project clears certain return thresholds.

Why do private funds exist in the first place?

They solve two problems at once.

For investors, they provide access to larger deals, professional management, and diversification that would be difficult to achieve individually. You may be able to buy a single rental house or invest in a handful of stocks, but you're unlikely to personally assemble a $20 million apartment development. Private funds make that possible by pooling capital.

For managers, private funds provide a practical mechanism to raise money from multiple sources and deploy it efficiently. Without pooled structures, most large-scale real estate projects and private equity investments simply wouldn't happen.

It's worth emphasizing that private funds are not some exotic Wall Street invention. They are, in many ways, the oldest and most natural form of investing: a group of people pooling their money together to take on opportunities larger than any one of them could pursue alone. What has changed in the modern era is the legal and regulatory framework that governs how these funds are formed, who can participate, and how they must be managed.

There's one other aspect of private funds that investors must understand. Earlier, I mentioned the similarities between private funds and more familiar fund types, such as mutual funds and ETFs, with the key difference that private funds are not publicly traded. This lack of liquidity is one of the biggest trade-offs. Private fund investors can't typically cash out at will, which introduces liquidity risk. Traditionally, this illiquidity has been compensated with the potential for higher returns.

This is the world that QOFs fit into.

At their core, QOFs are private funds, governed by the same dynamics and legal frameworks as any other pooled investment vehicle. What makes them unique, and what we'll explore next, is their special tax status under the Opportunity Zone program. But before we turn to those specifics, it's helpful to understand the classic relationship between the people who run a fund and the people who invest in it: the general partner and the limited partners.

GP/LP Structure Explained

Most private funds, including QOFs, are built on a GP/LP structure. GP stands for general partner, and LP stands for limited partner. Understanding this relationship is foundational to understanding how any private fund operates.

The general partner is the active investor and manager of the fund. This is the individual or team responsible for sourcing deals, deploying capital, overseeing operations, and making critical decisions—what to invest in, how to finance it, when to sell, and how to manage assets along the way. The GP has fiduciary responsibility to the investors, which means acting in their best interest, even while earning fees or a share of profits for their work.

The limited partners are the passive investors. They contribute capital but take no part in day-to-day management. Their liability is also limited: they can lose their investment, but not more. LPs are not personally responsible for any of the fund's debts or obligations beyond the capital they've committed.

Here's a simple analogy: think of the fund as a bus.

The GP is the driver, while the LPs are the passengers. They decide whether to get on, and which bus to board, but once they're seated, the GP controls the route, makes the stops, and determines when the journey ends. The LPs benefit from a successful trip, but they don't have their hands on the wheel.

This division of roles also explains how compensation is structured. LPs typically put up the majority of the capital and expect a return. GPs contribute expertise and time and are compensated in two primary ways: through management fees (which fund ongoing operations) and carried interest (also known as "carry" or "sponsor promote"), which is a share of the profits if the fund performs well.

Many GPs also invest their own capital into the fund. While their financial contribution is typically smaller than the LP pool, it carries symbolic weight. It shows alignment.

Suppose a $50 million fund is being raised. The GP contributes $5 million, which is 10 percent of the total equity, while LPs provide the remaining $45 million. That $5 million doesn't shift control (the GP still runs the fund), but it signals that the GP has skin in the game. If the project underperforms, the GP's capital is at risk, just like the investors'. If the fund succeeds, the GP wins not just from fees and sponsor promote, but also as a true co-investor.

This structure is not unique to Opportunity Zones. It's the standard model for private equity, venture capital, and real estate syndications. In fact, single-asset QOFs are simply real estate syndications wrapped in the OZ structure. The underlying relationship remains the same: GPs manage, LPs invest.

While LPs don't have a voice in daily decisions, they typically retain limited governance rights, as defined in each fund's operating agreement. For example, they may vote on major amendments to fund documents, approve GP replacements, or weigh in on certain liquidity events. But these rights are intentionally narrow. The GP/LP model works precisely because it draws a clear line between capital provision and decision-making—then aligns both sides through incentives and shared risk.

When structured correctly, it's a partnership in the truest sense: vision and execution on one side, trust and capital on the other.

How Private Funds Operate

Now that we've covered the GP/LP structure, let's explore how private funds actually function in the real world, from raising capital to managing distributions.

It all starts with fundraising. The general partner (or sponsor) prepares offering documents, markets the opportunity to prospective investors, and secures capital commitments. In a typical private equity or real estate fund, investors sign a subscription agreement pledging a specific amount of capital. Alongside this, they receive the fund's operating agreement, which outlines governance, profit-sharing, and management terms; and the Private Placement Memorandum (PPM), which discloses the investment's risks. These documents serve as the legal and informational foundation of the investor-GP relationship.

Once commitments are locked in, most private funds operate through capital calls.

Instead of collecting 100 percent of committed capital upfront, the GP calls capital incrementally, only when it's needed. For example, an investor who commits $1 million might wire $200,000 at acquisition, another $300,000 during construction, and the remainder later for improvements or reserves. This staggered model keeps idle cash to a minimum and allows investors to keep their uncalled capital working elsewhere until it's required.

Opportunity Zone funds are the exception.

Because investors must reinvest their capital gains within a strict 180-day window, most QOFs require full funding at the time of subscription. This ensures compliance with the tax code and avoids missed deadlines. So, while capital calls are common in the broader private fund world, in the OZ space, "all in at subscription" is the norm.

Once capital is deployed and projects are underway, the fund begins producing cash flow.

Distributions to investors follow a structured order. First, the fund services any debt. Next, it covers ongoing operating expenses, sets aside reserves, and only then begins distributing profits to equity investors, typically following a waterfall structure.

A typical waterfall starts with a preferred return to LPs, ensuring they receive a baseline return before the GP shares in any upside.

Once that threshold is met, profits are split between the LPs and GP, often 80/20—80 percent to the LP investors, 20 percent to the GP. If the project performs well, the GP's share, known as carried interest, can be substantial.

In the meantime, the GP may also earn management fees, usually 1 percent to 2 percent of either committed or invested capital. Some sponsors also charge acquisition fees when deals are closed or disposition fees when assets are sold. These fees support the fund's operations, including staff, legal, compliance, and GP oversight.

Still, the real economic incentive for the GP lies in the carry.

That carried interest—the 20 percent share of profits after the preferred return—is what aligns the GP's performance with the investors' outcomes. If the fund underperforms, the GP earns only fees. If it overdelivers, both parties share in the upside.

This is the operating backbone of nearly every private fund: raise capital, structure the fund, deploy capital, generate returns, and share profits. It's the same framework that governs traditional real estate syndications, and it's the model that most QOFs follow.

OZ funds come with a few critical twists, though. And in the next chapter, we'll break those down.

What Is a Qualified Opportunity Fund?

A QOF is a private investment vehicle with a public policy twist. Its purpose? To deploy capital into Qualified Opportunity Zone Property and deliver the tax advantages of the OZ program to its investors.

Structurally, a QOF looks like any private fund. Most are formed as limited partnerships or limited liability companies and operate under a typical GP/LP framework. What sets them apart is their tax designation.

To qualify as a QOF, the entity must be treated as a partnership or corporation for federal tax purposes. Disregarded entities (e.g., single-member LLCs) aren't eligible. A QOF doesn't need pre-approval from the IRS. There's no application, no waiting period, and no official seal of approval.

Instead, QOFs merely self-certify by filing IRS Form 8996[100] with the fund's first tax return, electing Qualified Opportunity Fund status. From that point forward, the fund must file the same form each year to demonstrate continued compliance.

The most critical compliance hurdle? The 90 percent investment standard.

A QOF must maintain at least 90 percent of its assets in Qualified Opportunity Zone Property (QOZP). This standard is measured twice annually, at midyear and year-end. Miss the mark, and the fund risks penalties or worse: disqualification.

The compliance burden rests entirely with the fund sponsor. Self-certification offers simplicity, but it also demands precision and accountability.

So who forms these funds?

In practice, there are two primary groups. First are professional fund managers—real estate sponsors, private equity firms, or institutional operators—launching multi-asset QOFs or raising capital for a single, large-scale project. Second are investors, developers, and entrepreneurs forming self-directed, captive QOFs to deploy their own capital in a more customized way. Some use these entities to fund and operate their own deals directly. Others use them as bespoke investment vehicles, allocating capital into one or more OZ investments managed by third-party operators while retaining control over capital allocation.

Regardless of the model, the rule is the same: no QOF, no tax benefits. For an investor to defer or eliminate capital gains under the OZ program, their dollars must flow through a QOF.

At its core, a QOF isn't exotic or complex. It's a familiar legal structure wrapped in a specific tax election. What matters isn't the label; it's the execution. A compliant QOF that meets the rules and performs on the ground unlocks powerful tax advantages.

---

100. "Form 8996: Qualified Opportunity Fund," Internal Revenue Service, updated January 23, 2026, https://www.irs.gov/forms-pubs/about-form-8996

How QOFs Hold Assets

Once a QOF is formed, the next question is tactical: how does it actually hold its investments?

There are two primary structures: direct ownership and the two-tier model.

In the direct ownership approach, the QOF itself acquires and holds Qualified Opportunity Zone Property. For example, the fund might purchase land in a designated zone and develop it directly. This model is clean and simple. The QOF raises capital, buys property, and manages the project.

While it may be easy to understand, it's sometimes harder to execute.

That's because QOFs must maintain 90 percent of their assets in qualified property, measured twice per year. In a direct-ownership setup, that compliance burden sits squarely on the fund itself. For many sponsors, that's a steep hill to climb.

Which is why most QOFs operate under a two-tier structure.

In this structure, the QOF doesn't invest directly in property. Instead, it invests in a subsidiary, typically an LLC taxed as a partnership, that qualifies as a QOZB. The QOZB is the entity that owns and operates the actual project(s), whether it's a real estate development, a business, or both.

This structure offers two big advantages.

First, the compliance threshold is lower. A QOZB must ensure that 70 percent of its tangible property is located in an Opportunity Zone. That's a lighter lift than the 90 percent investment standard required at the QOF level.

Second, and perhaps more importantly, QOZBs can use a thirty-one-month working capital safe harbor. This IRS provision allows a QOZB to hold significant amounts of cash or working capital for up to thirty-one months (and sometimes longer) without falling out of compliance, so long as there's a written plan for how those funds will be used to acquire, develop, or improve Qualified Opportunity Zone Property.[101]

That's a game-changer for development projects and operating businesses, where capital needs to be staged and deployed over time. Without that safe harbor, compliance would be nearly impossible during the early phases of construction or business ramp-up.

In practice, nearly all OZ investment sponsors use the two-tier model. It adds a layer of complexity, two entities instead of one, but the benefits far outweigh the administrative overhead.

For passive LP investors, the structure may not be obvious. But behind the scenes, it's the backbone of compliance. It's what allows the fund to manage cash, phase projects, and maintain its eligibility for the Opportunity Zone tax benefits.

The bottom line: fund structure matters.

Whether a QOF holds assets directly or through a QOZB determines how the rules apply, how flexible the fund can be, and how well it delivers on the promise of the program.

Why Structure Matters for Compliance and Returns

In QOF investing, structure isn't just a technical detail; it's a foundational decision. It shapes how the fund operates, how risk is managed, and how investors ultimately get paid.

Let's start with compliance.

The right structure can make it significantly easier to meet the Opportunity Zone program's statutory requirements. A two-tier structure—where the QOF invests into a QOZB—unlocks key advantages: the 70 percent tangible property test and the thirty-one-month working capital safe harbor. These tools give sponsors time and flexibility to deploy capital in a compliant way.

In contrast, a direct-ownership QOF is held to a stricter standard. It must meet the 90 percent test at the fund level and lacks access to

101. Treas. Reg. § 1.1400Z2(d)-1

the safe harbor. For a capital-intensive project with phased deployment, that can create unnecessary friction or even risk noncompliance.

The stakes are high. Choose the wrong structure, or mismanage a compliant one, and the entire tax benefit can be jeopardized, not just for the sponsor, but for every investor in the fund.

Then there's the impact on returns.

Structure governs how money flows into and out of the fund, how fees are assessed, and how profits are split. A multi-asset QOF provides diversification and risk smoothing. A single-asset fund offers sharper focus but more exposure to any one project. A captive QOF gives full control, but only over deals that the investor can source and manage directly.

Even within a single project, the operating agreement defines the economics. Who gets paid first. How preferred returns are calculated. What happens once profit hurdles are cleared. Waterfall structures, fee layers, and terms of the sponsor promote all stem from fund design, not just from the project itself.

In other words, structure shapes outcomes.

A well-structured OZ investment can align interests, preserve compliance flexibility, and create a fair balance of risk and reward. A poorly structured one can do the opposite—skewing economics toward the sponsor, creating ambiguity in execution, or raising the risk of IRS scrutiny.

That's why diligence must extend beyond the pitch deck. It's not enough to evaluate the project. Investors must also understand how the fund itself is built because that's the vehicle that carries the investment, and the structure that determines whether it reaches its destination.

Structure isn't a footnote. It's the foundation.

CHAPTER EIGHT

SOURCING AND VETTING OZ INVESTMENTS

NOW IT'S TIME TO ASK A VERY PRACTICAL question: How do you actually find OZ investments worth making? And once a deal crosses your desk, how do you separate signal from noise—credible opportunities from costly distractions?

In Opportunity Zone investing, the deal matters just as much as the structure.

Where to Find OZ Investments

For most investors, the first challenge is knowing where to look.

The Opportunity Zone landscape is vast: thousands of Qualified Opportunity Funds (QOFs) and projects populate the market. But not all of them are accessible. And not all are worth your attention.

The key is to focus on channels that consistently produce credible, compliant, and investable opportunities.

THE OPPORTUNITYZONES.COM MARKETPLACE

One of the most efficient starting points is the OpportunityZones.com

Marketplace.[102] This platform was built to connect accredited investors with OZ sponsors in a curated, centralized hub.

Rather than relying on scattered introductions or word of mouth, the marketplace allows you to browse a wide range of offerings—ground-up multifamily developments, operating businesses, diversified funds—all in one place. Side-by-side comparisons help sharpen your sense of what's available and how different strategies stack up.

It streamlines discovery. And more importantly, it raises the signal-to-noise ratio.

OZ PITCH DAY EVENTS

Another powerful source of deal flow is our OZ Pitch Day series.[103] I launched the event in 2020, during a time when it was especially difficult for investors to access vetted OZ opportunities. The concept was simple: bring fund sponsors and investors together for a focused, high-quality deal showcase.

The response was immediate and overwhelming.

Since then, OZ Pitch Day has hosted more than 15,000 attendees and has helped raise untold millions in equity for participating funds. For investors, the format is both efficient and revealing. In just a few hours, you can hear from multiple sponsors, compare deals in real time, and ask direct questions live.

Attendees often tell me they walk away with not only viable investment opportunities but also a clearer understanding of what "good" looks like in an Opportunity Zone offering.

For me, OZ Pitch Day has become a highlight of my work in the Opportunity Zone space. There's an energy that builds when hundreds of investors gather to evaluate opportunities together. It's not just a showcase; it's a marketplace of ideas. And the relationships it sparks often extend far beyond the event itself.

---

102. You can browse our OZ Investment Marketplace at https://opportunityzones.com/marketplace/

103. We host multiple OZ Pitch Day events each year. Learn more: https://ozpitchday.com/

'SCALED-UP' SPONSORS

Some sponsors operate at a different level of scale.

While many credible OZ fund managers run lean teams and focus on one deal at a time, a handful of firms have built large, scalable OZ platforms. These "scaled-up" sponsors often work through financial advisor networks, including Registered Investment Advisors (RIAs) and broker-dealers. Some will also engage directly with individual investors.

Well-known names in this category include Bridge Investment Group, CIM, Cantor Fitzgerald, Griffin Capital, Origin Investments, Capital Square, and Caliber, to name a few. Their offerings often include multi-asset strategies, institutional-grade compliance, and broader geographic diversification.

SPONSOR NETWORKS AND REFERRALS

For experienced investors, the most consistent source of high-quality OZ deals is simple: trusted relationships.

Sponsors, fund managers, and developers with strong track records tend to surface through networks—yours or your advisors'. CPAs, attorneys, and wealth managers are often early to hear about capital raises and can steer you toward sponsors they trust.

Communities like OZ Insiders, my private Opportunity Zone mastermind group, create another layer of vetting, giving members direct access to peers who've already invested, who have already done due diligence on a sponsor, or who have walked away from a deal for a good reason.

Referrals aren't just faster; they're smarter.

INSTITUTIONAL ACCESS

If you're aligned with a family office, multi-family office, or large RIA, you may gain access to institutional OZ funds.

These are typically multi-asset vehicles with broad pipelines, high compliance standards, and higher minimums. While not available to everyone, institutional access can unlock exposure to sophisticated deals that never show up on public platforms or retail marketing channels.

The bottom line: great OZ deals aren't found by accident.

They're sourced through intentional channels: platforms, events, networks, and relationships designed to surface real opportunities and filter out the noise.

As an investor, your edge comes from knowing where to look and whom to trust when you get there.

Once you understand where to find Opportunity Zone investments, you need to recognize the three primary structures through which investors typically access the market, each with distinct risk-return profiles:

- Single-asset developer deals offer clarity and alignment around a specific project, but carry concentrated asset-level risk.
- Institutional multi-asset funds pool capital across diversified portfolios with professional management, offering broader diversification but often with higher minimums and less transparency into individual investments.
- Self-directed, or captive, QOFs allow investors, families, or closely held groups to create their own fund structure and deploy capital according to their own strategy—whether into their own projects, third-party sponsored deals, or a customized portfolio of OZ investments. This approach offers maximum control and customization but also introduces additional administrative complexity and responsibility.

The right choice depends on aligning the structure with your specific goals, risk tolerance, and investing style, whether diversified or concentrated, sponsor-led or self-directed.

Evaluating Deals for Compliance and Returns

Once you've identified a potential Opportunity Zone investment, the next step is due diligence.

This is where strategy meets scrutiny, where you determine not just whether a deal qualifies for OZ tax treatment, but whether it stands on its own as a sound investment.

STEP 1. START WITH COMPLIANCE

The first filter is always compliance.

If a deal isn't properly structured under OZ rules, nothing else matters. Tax benefits are earned, not assumed, and there's no room for sloppiness here.

Begin with the basics:

- Has the entity self-certified with the IRS as a QOF?
- Is the investment structured directly at the QOF level, or is it routed through a QOZB?

Both approaches are permissible, but they carry different compliance burdens. Understanding which structure is being used and how it's being implemented is essential. We'll unpack those distinctions further in Part III.

If the sponsor can't clearly explain how the structure satisfies OZ eligibility, that's your cue to walk away.

STEP 2. FOCUS ON RETURN DRIVERS

Once compliance is confirmed, the analysis shifts to returns and the assumptions behind them. This is where real diligence begins.

For real estate, key return drivers include:

- Rent growth: Are projected rents realistic? Or is the sponsor assuming aggressive jumps that outpace the submarket's historical trend?
- Occupancy and absorption: How quickly is the property expected to lease up? Is there enough sustained demand to hit those targets?
- Exit cap rates: A seemingly minor cap rate adjustment at exit can swing the Internal Rate of Return (IRR) dramatically. Conservative assumptions matter. An overly optimistic exit cap may look good on paper, but it spells trouble in real life.

For operating businesses, the focus shifts to growth and scalability:

- Revenue Trajectory: Is the top-line growth backed by a real go-to-market strategy? Or is it just wishful modeling?
- Margins: Are the unit economics strong? Can the business withstand pricing pressure, rising costs, or economic turbulence?
- Scalability: Does the model scale beyond a single OZ location? Or is it bound by geography?

Whether it's bricks or businesses, these variables shape your return profile. They also reveal whether the sponsor is operating with rigor, or just reverse-engineering numbers to hit a target IRR.

STEP 3. ASSESS RETURN EXPECTATIONS AND REALITY CHECKS

So what's reasonable?

For real estate, a common return benchmark is an IRR in the mid-to-high teens and a 2x to 3x multiple on invested capital over a ten-year hold. These are not guarantees. They are directional guides to help you gauge whether a pro forma is grounded in reality or floating on best-case assumptions.

The key is this: Do the numbers make sense? Are the projections backed by data, experience, and market fundamentals? Or do they require flawless execution, perfect timing, and heroic assumptions just to break even?

STEP 4. DON'T LET THE (TAX) TAIL WAG THE DOG

The mistake many investors make is letting the tax benefit override weak fundamentals. But the OZ incentive was never meant to rescue bad deals. It was designed to *enhance* good ones, to tip the scale, not to rebuild it from scratch.

As Jim Lang, a corporate and tax attorney at Greenberg Traurig, puts it, "It's important for any fund sponsor to have the flexibility to adjust to the market and not let the proverbial 'tax tail wag the business dog.'"[104]

---

104. Jim Lang (attorney at Greenberg Traurig), via email with the author, February 6, 2026.

The strongest Opportunity Zone projects start as sound investments, before you even factor in the tax benefits. The fundamentals need to be there: realistic rents, credible growth, and experienced sponsors. The OZ incentive then becomes the differentiator—the reason a deal that was merely OK becomes investable, and a deal that was investable becomes compelling.

In other words, tax advantages don't replace performance. They reward it.

What Documents to Expect

Once you've identified a promising Opportunity Zone investment, the next step is document review. This isn't just paperwork; it's due diligence in action. These materials help you understand the opportunity, assess the sponsor, and confirm that the offering meets professional standards.

If these documents are incomplete, vague, or missing entirely, that's a red flag.

PITCH DECK AND EXECUTIVE SUMMARY

The first document you'll likely receive is the pitch deck. This is the sponsor's executive overview, their chance to explain the investment thesis, highlight the project's strengths, and introduce the team. Sometimes the executive summary is a separate document. Sometimes it's embedded directly into the deck.

Either way, it should answer the big questions:

- What is the sponsor building or operating?
- Why does the deal make sense—economically, strategically, and geographically?
- What kind of returns are they targeting?

The pitch deck is not the place for legal fine print or exhaustive financials. It's a high-level introduction. But it should be clear, compelling, and professionally presented. If it feels rushed, shallow, or vague, that's an early signal that the sponsor may not be ready for capital investment.

PRIVATE PLACEMENT MEMORANDUM (PPM)

The heavy lift comes in the Private Placement Memorandum (PPM). This is the core legal disclosure document for most private offerings. Its job is simple: disclose all material facts and allocate risk to the investor.

A well-constructed PPM should include:

- a full description of the offering;
- sponsor responsibilities and compensation;
- potential conflicts of interest;
- fees and expenses;
- investment risk factors and disclaimers;
- legal structure and governance; and
- market analysis and financial projections (sometimes included).

Crucially, the offering's operating agreement, subscription agreement, pitch deck, website, and other marketing materials, as well as verbal statements made by the sponsor, should be consistent with the PPM.

The PPM doesn't sugarcoat the downside; it's meant to protect the sponsor legally by disclosing all material risks. For the investor, it's a critical tool for understanding exactly what you're signing up for.

If a sponsor doesn't have a PPM or provides one that feels boilerplate or incomplete, proceed with caution. Professional sponsors (and their legal counsel) treat this document as essential.

SUBSCRIPTION DOCUMENTS

When you're ready to invest, you'll receive a subscription package. This is the legal set of documents that binds you to the investment. It usually includes:

- a subscription agreement, where you state your investment amount and accept the terms;
- an accredited investor questionnaire, required for compliance with securities regulations;

- a personal information form, typically for Anti-Money Laundering (AML)[105] and Know Your Customer (KYC)[106] compliance;
- wiring instructions for transferring your capital to the QOF; and
- the fund's operating agreement or limited partnership agreement, outlining governance, voting rights, and profit distributions.

These documents formalize your commitment and define your relationship to the fund. They're not optional, and they shouldn't be vague.

WHY IT MATTERS

If a sponsor cannot provide these three materials—pitch deck (and/or executive summary), a PPM, and subscription documents—you should stop there. These are the baseline expectations for any credible offering. Without them, you're operating without a roadmap, without a risk disclosure, and without a legal agreement defining your rights.

And in a program like Opportunity Zones, where timing, compliance, and long-term structure matter, those gaps are unacceptable.

Common Red Flags and Deal-Killers

Not every OZ investment is worth your time or your capital. Some will fail the sniff test right out of the gate. Others may look promising on the surface but unravel under scrutiny.

Knowing what to watch for can save you time, protect your capital, and keep you focused on credible opportunities.

1. WEAK TRACK RECORD OR SPONSOR EVASION

The most critical filter in OZ investing is sponsor quality. A sponsor without a meaningful track record, or one unwilling to share it,

---

105. Will Kenton, "Understanding Anti-Money Laundering (AML): Key Processes and Global Impact," Investopedia, August 16, 2025, https://www.investopedia.com/terms/a/aml.asp

106. James Chen, "Know Your Client (KYC): Key Requirements and Compliance for Financial Services," Investopedia, August 28, 2025, https://www.investopedia.com/terms/k/knowyourclient.asp

should raise immediate concern. Every developer or entrepreneur starts somewhere, but asking investors to commit millions without demonstrating prior success is a big ask.

Even worse: evasiveness. If a sponsor dodges questions about past projects, glosses over details, or resists transparency, walk away. You're not just betting on a business plan, you're betting on the people executing it.

Bottom line: if there's one set of deal-breakers to prioritize, it's track record and transparency.

2. UNREALISTIC PROJECTIONS

Another red flag is overly rosy financial modeling. If a sponsor promises high returns with little explanation, or worse, uses words like "guaranteed," it's time to move on.

In real estate and private equity, there are no guarantees. Responsible sponsors present realistic assumptions that are grounded in market comps, credible absorption rates, and defensible exit cap rates. They don't build pro formas based on best-case scenarios stacked end to end.

Your job is to pressure-test those assumptions. If they don't hold up, neither will the deal.

3. EXCESSIVE FEES OR MISALIGNED INCENTIVES

Fees are part of the private fund landscape. But they must be aligned with investor success.

If a sponsor structures the deal so they get paid regardless of performance, or front-loads fees that extract value before anything's been delivered, that's a warning sign.

Look for balance:

- management fees should cover operating costs, not serve as profit centers;
- acquisition and disposition fees should be reasonable; and
- promote structures (carried interest) should reward performance, not entitlement.

If the deal seems tilted in the sponsor's favor before the first dollar is invested, it's not a partnership. It's a transaction, and one you're likely to regret.

4. COMPLIANCE SHORTCUTS

Opportunity Zones come with strict compliance requirements. Any sponsor who dismisses them, downplays them, or can't clearly explain how they'll meet them is a liability.

Whether it's the 90 percent asset test, the substantial improvement rule, or the mechanics of a QOZB, a professional sponsor should know these cold or be surrounded by advisors who do.

You don't want to be the one left holding the bag if the IRS comes knocking. If the compliance roadmap isn't clear, keep moving.

5. MISSING OR SLOPPY DOCUMENTS

As covered in the previous section, credible deals come with a complete, professionally prepared document suite:

- pitch deck or executive summary;
- Private Placement Memorandum (PPM); and a
- subscription package, including agreement, questionnaire, and legal docs.

These aren't optional. They're baseline requirements for any serious capital raise. If these materials are absent or poorly assembled, it's not just a red flag. It's a deal-killer. So, if you encounter one or more of these red flags, don't negotiate. Don't rationalize. Just walk away.

There's no shortage of strong, well-prepared OZ sponsors in the marketplace—teams who understand the rules, model returns responsibly, and approach capital with professionalism and respect. Let them earn your investment. Don't let tax benefits blind you to flaws that would disqualify the same deal if it weren't in an Opportunity Zone.

When in doubt, pass. In OZ investing, discipline isn't just wise. It's essential.

Balancing Tax Benefits with Fundamentals

One of the most critical dynamics in Opportunity Zone investing is the interplay between fundamentals and tax benefits. The OZ incentive is powerful, but it's not a substitute for a sound investment thesis. It's an amplifier, not a savior.

Plenty of OZ deals are solid on their own. A multifamily project in a growing submarket, for example, might produce respectable returns even without the tax overlay. But layer in the OZ benefits, and suddenly the math changes. What was good becomes compelling.

That's exactly the point.

The Opportunity Zone program was never designed to subsidize failing ideas. It was built to tip the scale—to bridge the gap for projects that almost pencil, that serve a public purpose, and that need just a little more to become viable for private capital. In those cases, the incentive works exactly as intended.

But it only works when the fundamentals are sound. The OZ tax incentive cannot fix poor underwriting, a bad location, or an inexperienced sponsor. Nor can it compensate for weak demand, flawed execution, or thin margins. If the foundation is cracked, it doesn't matter how generous the tax treatment is.

A bad deal is still a bad deal.

That's why investors must approach OZ deals with discipline, starting with fundamentals, then layering on tax strategy.

Evaluate the underwriting assumptions. Are rent projections reasonable? Is absorption realistic? Are operating margins defensible? Does the sponsor have the capability to execute?

Then and only then factor in the Opportunity Zone benefits.

Also, remember to view everything on an after-fee, after-tax basis. That's the real number that matters. If a sponsor is projecting a 17 percent IRR or a 2.5x multiple on invested capital (MOIC), ask: What's left after management fees, promote splits, and taxes? How much of that return actually reaches your pocket?

The OZ incentive should be the icing, not the cake.

When the fundamentals are strong, and the tax treatment enhances—not masks—the economics, you've got a real opportunity. That's when OZ investing shines: solid returns, amplified by long-term tax efficiency, aligned with community impact.

That's the zone you want to be in.

Advisor and CPA Role in Due Diligence

Opportunity Zone investing should never be a solo endeavor.

Even if you have years of experience, you'll benefit from the insight of trusted advisors—professionals who can spot risks, challenge assumptions, and ensure that your investment is structured for both compliance and performance.

That's not just helpful. It's essential.

One of the recurring themes throughout this book is that OZ investing is about structure as much as strategy. That means surrounding yourself with the right team, especially when it comes to tax and compliance.

STEP 1. START WITH YOUR CPA

Your CPA should be one of the first calls you make before wiring funds. Their role isn't just tax preparation; it's strategic.

A qualified CPA can help you:

- evaluate how an OZ investment fits into your broader tax picture;
- analyze how it interacts with other strategies (1031 exchanges, Roth conversions, charitable trusts, etc.);
- model after-tax returns—the only numbers that ultimately matter; and
- clarify what reporting will be required, including Form 8997 and other key filings.

This level of planning can significantly impact your outcome. A good CPA won't just help you stay compliant; they'll help you optimize.

STEP 2. DO YOU NEED AN ATTORNEY?

In most cases, no, you don't need a lawyer to review every OZ deal you consider. The exception is if you're forming your own QOF. In that case, hiring a tax attorney is non-negotiable. You'll need help with:

- fund formation and operating agreements;
- QOF self-certification;
- structuring for QOZB eligibility, if applicable; and
- SEC compliance (if raising capital from others).

STEP 3. LOOP IN YOUR FINANCIAL ADVISOR

Your financial advisor or wealth manager can offer critical portfolio-level insight. They'll help you assess whether the OZ investment:

- aligns with your broader asset allocation;
- fits your liquidity needs and time horizon;
- matches your risk profile and return expectations.

Remember: OZ deals are long-term and illiquid. They don't belong in every portfolio. A good advisor can help you keep the big picture in view.

STEP 4. TAP INTO PEER NETWORKS

Professional advice is vital. But don't underestimate the value of peer insight.

Other investors, especially those who've invested in similar deals or worked with the same sponsor, can offer candid, experience-based feedback you won't find in a pitch deck. Communities like our OZ Insiders mastermind bring together active investors, sponsors, and advisors.[107] Members compare notes, and share sponsor intel and surface opportunities—and red flags—you might otherwise miss.

In a landscape as specialized as Opportunity Zones, these peer insights can be just as valuable as professional counsel.

---

107. For more information about OZ Insiders, visit https://ozinsiders.com/

STEP 5. MAKE IT A TEAM SPORT

At its best, Opportunity Zone investing is a collaborative effort. Surround yourself with the right professionals, engage with informed peers, and lean on the collective wisdom of others who've walked this path before.

You'll not only avoid costly mistakes, but you'll also move forward with confidence, knowing your investment is structured correctly from day one.

Building a Personal OZ Deal Flow Pipeline

The most successful OZ investors don't operate deal-to-deal. They operate from a pipeline.

When you have multiple deals in front of you, everything sharpens. You see what's standard. You recognize what's exceptional. And most importantly, you avoid being boxed into a one-off opportunity that doesn't truly fit.

Building that kind of consistent deal flow takes intention, but it's entirely within reach.

LEVERAGE THE RIGHT PLATFORMS

A smart first step is to plug into curated deal platforms. Subscribing to the OpportunityZones.com newsletter ensures a steady stream of projects and funds lands in your inbox. It's efficient, it's diverse, and it gives you early exposure to sponsors you might otherwise never meet.

Attending recurring events like OZ Pitch Day[108] is another high-leverage move. Each event introduces a new set of private investment opportunities and provides direct access to sponsors, often including live Q&A. Show up regularly and, over time, you'll develop both deal familiarity and sponsor familiarity.

---

108. For more information about OZ Pitch Day, visit https://ozpitchday.com/

BUILD SPONSOR RELATIONSHIPS

Relationships drive access. A sponsor you meet today may not have a current deal that fits, but staying in touch puts you on the short list when the right one comes along.

Over time, that casual conversation turns into a pipeline. You'll start to see projects earlier, with more context, and sometimes with better terms. It's not just networking; it's positioning.

TAP INTO INVESTOR COMMUNITIES

Peer networks matter.

Communities like OZ Insiders give you access to fellow investors who are actively evaluating deals, trading insights, and sharing referrals. These groups can provide opportunities that never hit public platforms, and give you candid feedback on sponsors, structures, and performance.

When someone in your network says, "We invested with this group last year; here's what you need to know," that kind of insight is invaluable.

MOVE FROM REACTING TO MANAGING

The ultimate goal is to stop reacting to individual deals and start managing a pipeline.

When deals come to you consistently, you're not stuck evaluating one offering in a vacuum. You can:

- compare returns and assumptions side by side;
- spot which sponsors consistently show up prepared; and
- say "no" without regret, because another deal is already in the queue.

This shift changes everything. You move from being deal-hungry to deal-selective. From passive recipient to informed gatekeeper.

That's how you play the long game in Opportunity Zone investing, and how you stack the odds in your favor.

So now that you know what strong deals look like from the outside, it's time to learn how to build them from the inside.

PART III

THE FUND AND DEAL SPONSOR PLAYBOOK

CHAPTER NINE

HOW TO LAUNCH A QUALIFIED OPPORTUNITY FUND

THIS CHAPTER MARKS A TURNING POINT in the book.

Until now, we've approached Opportunity Zones from the investor's side, but now we are shifting perspectives. The focus now moves to the sponsor, the person or team responsible for creating and managing a Qualified Opportunity Fund (QOF).

Launching a QOF may sound complex, but it doesn't have to be. At its core, a QOF is simply a non-disregarded corporation or partnership[109] that self-certifies with the IRS and complies with the program's rules. Most commonly, it's structured as an LLC taxed as a partnership, but some QOFs take the form of C corporations or Real Estate Investment Trusts (REITs).

From that basic framework, the range of fund structures spans from simple, single-asset entities created to house one person's capital gain to sophisticated, multi-asset funds with hundreds or thousands of investors.

109. A non-disregarded entity is a business entity that is treated as a separate taxable entity from its owner by the IRS. Notably, a single-member LLC is a disregarded entity. Even though it may have its own unique taxpayer ID, for all intents and purposes, the IRS disregards it, as all of its income merely passes through to its single member owner. Thus, a single-member LLC cannot be a QOF.

The purpose of this chapter is to walk you through that entire spectrum. If you're raising capital from other investors, we'll also cover the additional legal documentation and investor protections required under securities laws.

Captive QOF vs. Professionally Managed Fund

The first decision in launching a QOF is whether you're creating a captive vehicle or a professionally managed, investor-facing fund. This choice defines not how large the fund will be or how many assets it will hold, but who the capital comes from, and what obligations come with it.

A captive QOF (also referred to as a self-directed QOF) is created when an individual, developer, or business owner uses their own eligible gain to invest in qualifying assets. There are no outside investors, no need to market a securities offering, and no requirement for a formal suite of investor documents.

This structure offers simplicity, speed, and control. A captive QOF can be small and narrowly focused or large and complex. It might hold a single property or multiple projects. The defining feature isn't the size, it's the capital source: entirely internal.

As corporate and tax attorney Jim Lang of Greenberg Traurig explains, "A captive Qualified Opportunity Fund is rather efficient to establish, and attention to funding and deployment timelines is likely the highest risk, besides actually finding good QOZB eligible deals or projects."[110]

By contrast, a professionally managed fund is built to raise capital from third parties. That one decision changes everything. Now you're in the realm of:

- securities law compliance;
- Private Placement Memoranda (PPMs);
- subscription documents and investor onboarding; and
- ongoing investor reporting and governance.

---

110. Lang, email.

These funds can also be single-asset or multi-asset, focused or diversified. What distinguishes them is not structure or scope, but the presence of outside limited partners, and the corresponding duty to act as fiduciary and manage their capital with transparency, accountability, and operational rigor.

It's important to note: neither structure limits your ambition.

A captive QOF can scale just as large as a professionally managed one (provided it has the necessary capital). Likewise, an investor-facing fund can focus on a single project just as easily as it can pursue a diversified portfolio.

The real distinction is this: Are you investing your own capital or managing capital on behalf of others?

That decision shapes everything that follows.

Single-Asset vs. Multi-Asset QOF Formation

Once you've decided whether your QOF will be captive or offered to outside investors, the next step is determining whether it will be a single-asset or multi-asset fund. This choice defines how capital will be deployed—into one specific deal, or across a portfolio—and it carries meaningful implications for diversification and risk management.

A single-asset QOF is structured to hold just one investment—either a property or an operating business. For sponsors with a specific project in mind, this is often the cleanest and most efficient approach. The entity exists for one purpose, and all capital flows into a single deal.

For example:

- A developer might form a QOF solely to fund the ground-up construction of a multifamily project in a Qualified Opportunity Zone.
- A business owner might launch a QOF to finance a new startup business located in a zone.

If third-party investors are involved, the pitch is simple: "This fund owns this project."

The downside? Concentration risk.

If that one project struggles or fails, there's no other investment to soften the blow. For captive funds, that risk may be acceptable, especially when the sponsor is directly managing the asset. But in a professionally managed QOF with outside investors, this risk must be disclosed and underwritten carefully.

By contrast, a multi-asset QOF is built to invest in multiple projects. That could mean:

- geographic diversification across cities or states;
- sector diversification (e.g., a fund that deploys capital into housing, industrial, and business investments); or
- multiple properties within the same market and asset class.

Even a narrowly focused strategy—say, all multifamily developments in Nashville—benefits from the ability to spread capital across several timelines and outcomes. That diversification is a defining feature of the multi-asset structure.

From a legal and compliance standpoint, the mechanics of both approaches are similar, but from an operational standpoint, the complexity is different. A single-asset QOF is relatively simple to manage. A multi-asset fund requires more infrastructure, detailed accounting, and clear investor communication to manage multiple assets simultaneously.

There's no one-size-fits-all answer.

- If you're focused on a specific project and want a clean, streamlined vehicle, a single-asset QOF may be ideal.
- If you're seeking risk mitigation or plan to raise capital for a portfolio strategy, a multi-asset QOF gives you the structure to deliver it.

The right structure depends on your goals, your capital base, and the level of operational complexity you're prepared to manage.

Checklist of Essentials for Every QOF

Whether you're forming a captive fund or a professionally managed one, every QOF must follow a core set of steps. These are the

Form **8996** (Rev. December 2021) Department of the Treasury Internal Revenue Service

Qualified Opportunity Fund

► Go to *www.irs.gov/Form8996* for instructions and the latest information.
► Attach to your tax return. See instructions.

OMB No. 1545-0123
Attachment Sequence No. **996**

Name | **Employer identification number**

Part I General Information and Certification

1 Type of taxpayer: ☐ Corporation ☐ Partnership

2 Is the taxpayer organized for the purpose of investing in qualified opportunity zone (QOZ) property (other than another qualified opportunity fund (QOF))?
☐ **No. STOP.** Do not file this form with your tax return.
☐ **Yes.** Go to line 3.

3 Is this the first period the taxpayer is a QOF?
☐ **Yes.** By checking this box, you certify that by the end of the taxpayer's first QOF year, the taxpayer's organizing documents include a statement of the entity's purpose of investing in QOZ property and a description of the trade or business(es) that the QOF is engaged in either directly or through a QOZ business. See instructions.
☐ **No.**

4 If you checked "Yes" on line 3, provide the first month in which the fund chose to be a QOF . . . . ► ________

5 Did any investor dispose of, in part or in whole, their equity interest in the fund?
☐ **Yes.** Attach a statement with each investor's name, the date of disposal, and the interest that they transferred during the QOF's tax year.
☐ **No.**

6 ☐ Do not check this box. Reserved for future use.

Part II Investment Standard Calculation

7	Enter the amount from Part VI, line 2, for total QOZ property held by the taxpayer on the last day of the first 6-month period of the taxpayer's tax year. See instructions if Part I, line 3, is "Yes"	7	
8	Total assets held by the taxpayer on the last day of the first 6-month period of the taxpayer's tax year. See instructions if Part I, line 3, is "Yes"	8	
9	Divide line 7 by line 8	9	
10	Enter the amount from Part VI, line 3, for total QOZ property held by the taxpayer on the last day of the taxpayer's tax year	10	
11	Total assets held by the taxpayer on the last day of the taxpayer's tax year	11	

IRS Form 8996 is filed annually by Qualified Opportunity Funds.

foundational elements. Skip them, and your fund risks falling out of compliance before it begins.

Think of this as your launch checklist.

1. ENTITY FORMATION

Every QOF must be a non-disregarded legal entity, typically an LLC taxed as a partnership, though C corporations and REITs are also permitted.

The entity must be organized under US law and remain in good standing in its state of formation.

2. EIN AND BANK ACCOUNTS

Once the entity is formed, apply for an Employer Identification Number (EIN) from the IRS. Then, open a new bank account.

Do not commingle QOF capital with other funds or business operations. Keeping OZ equity separate is one of the simplest ways to maintain clear records and avoid compliance issues down the line.

3. IRS SELF-CERTIFICATION

QOFs do not need pre-approval from the IRS. Instead, they self-certify by filing Form 8996 with their first tax return, and again every year thereafter.

This is not a formality. The self-certification carries the force of law, and the burden of proof is entirely on the fund. As the fund manager, you are responsible for compliance from day one and every year thereafter.

4. OPERATING AGREEMENT

Every fund needs a governing document. For an LLC, this is typically the entity's Operating Agreement.

This agreement defines:

- who controls the fund;
- how decisions are made;
- how profits and losses are allocated; and
- what rights the limited partners have.

Even for a captive QOF, it's best practice to formalize the structure with a written agreement. It reinforces legitimacy, supports tax documentation, and provides clarity for future audits or capital events.

5. OZ ELIGIBILITY CONFIRMATION (BEFORE DEPLOYING CAPITAL)

Before a QOF deploys any capital, the sponsor must confirm that the investment qualifies for Opportunity Zone treatment. This step is foundational. If the asset is not eligible, no amount of structuring or compliance can cure the defect later.

First, verify that the property or operating business is located within a designated Opportunity Zone. This requires confirming that the specific parcel or business address falls inside an officially designated census tract, using a reliable Opportunity Zone map.[111] This determination should be documented and retained.

---

111. OpportunityZones.com maintains a map: https://opportunityzones.com/map/

Next, confirm that the intended use is eligible. Certain "sin businesses"[112] are expressly excluded from Opportunity Zone treatment. Confirm that the activity constitutes an active trade or business rather than a passive investment. Confirm that the project can satisfy the original use or substantial improvement requirements.

For operating businesses, confirm that the business model can meet the Qualified Opportunity Zone Business tests on an ongoing basis.

Finally, document the eligibility analysis. This can be as simple as a retained map screenshot or a short internal memo explaining why the asset qualifies. The key is being able to demonstrate, years later if necessary, that eligibility was evaluated and confirmed before capital was deployed.

6. THE 90 PERCENT ASSET TEST

Every QOF must comply with the 90 percent asset test.

Twice each year, the fund must prove that at least 90 of its assets are invested in Qualified Opportunity Zone Property (QOZP). This requires:

- accurate investment tracking;
- timely testing on the required semiannual dates; and
- documentation that can withstand scrutiny.

Many sponsors hire third-party administrators to assist with testing and reporting. Your CPA may be able to assist with this as well. But even for small, self-managed QOFs, the obligation is the same: you must be able to prove compliance.

7. PROFESSIONAL TEAM

A QOF isn't just an entity. It's a functioning structure. At a minimum, you'll need:

---

112. This is discussed in more detail in Chapter 6. Per IRC § 144(c)(6)(B), the list of sin businesses includes golf courses, country clubs, massage parlors, hot tub facilities, tanning facilities, racetracks or other facilities used for gambling, and liquor stores.

- a CPA who understands Opportunity Zone rules and Form 8996 compliance;
- legal counsel for entity formation and fund structuring (if raising outside capital, a securities attorney is essential);
- a fund administrator or bookkeeper to maintain records and prepare compliance reports; and
- if you're raising significant outside capital, a marketing executive, placement agent, or managing broker-dealer may be required to assist with investor sourcing and regulatory compliance.

8. OFFERING DOCUMENTS (IF RAISING CAPITAL)

If you're accepting money from outside investors, you're entering the world of securities offerings. That means preparing:

- a Private Placement Memorandum (PPM);
- subscription agreements; and
- investor questionnaires.

These documents:

- disclose risk;
- outline the fund's business plan and structure;
- confirm investor suitability and accreditation; and
- protect you as the issuer by clarifying terms and expectations.

Without them, you expose yourself to legal and regulatory risk and create ambiguity that can derail investor relationships.

Whether your QOF is small and simple or large and institutional, these are the non-negotiables. Get them right at the outset, and you'll avoid the most common pitfalls that derail funds before they ever get off the ground.

Intro to QOZBs: The Two-Tier Structure

One of the most important structural decisions when launching a QOF is whether the fund will own assets directly or invest through a subsidiary entity known as a Qualified Opportunity Zone Business (QOZB).

In practice, most funds choose the two-tiered approach:

- the QOF sits at the top; and
- the QOZB or QOZBs operate underneath it, owning and managing the actual asset(s) or business(es).

This structure isn't just common; it's strategic. Now, why does the two-tier system exist? The answer comes down to compliance flexibility.

At the QOF level, the IRS requires that 90 percent of assets be invested in Qualified Opportunity Zone Property (QOZP). That's a high bar. However, when the QOF invests through a QOZB, the subsidiary is allowed more leeway: only 70 percent of the QOZB's tangible property must be located in the Opportunity Zone.

That twenty-point difference is often the deciding factor. It creates breathing room. It allows for functional, real-world operations while still staying compliant.

Here's the typical flow:

1. an investor realizes a capital gain;
2. the investor rolls that gain into a QOF;
3. the QOF contributes the capital into one or more QOZBs; and
4. the QOZB(s) use the funds to develop one or more projects or run one or more businesses in the Opportunity Zone.

This model applies across sectors:

- In real estate, the QOZB owns the property, hires contractors, manages construction, and oversees leasing.
- In an operating business, the QOZB is the company itself carrying out day-to-day activities inside the zone.

Beyond compliance, the two-tier structure offers real operational benefits:

- liability separation between the fund and the project;
- easier ability to raise debt at the project level;

- simpler accounting and reporting, as operations are confined to a single subsidiary;
- ability to take advantage of a thirty-one-month working capital safe harbor (more detail on this topic in Chapter 12); and the
- ability to raise money from other QOFs (as they can invest in your QOZB[s]).

These advantages explain why even though QOFs are technically permitted to hold assets directly, very few do.

The two-tier model has become the default structure for good reason. It offers flexibility, protection, and a compliance path that works in the real world.

Additional Requirements If Raising Outside Capital

If your QOF is designed to deploy only your own capital, the setup can be lean: form the entity, open a bank account, file Form 8996, and ensure compliance with the 90 percent asset test.

However, the moment you invite outside investors into your fund, you cross into a different regulatory landscape. You're no longer just an investor. You're now an issuer of securities, and that change brings significant legal, operational, and compliance responsibilities. More on this in Chapter 10.

INVESTOR COMMUNICATIONS

Outside investors expect, and are legally entitled to, clear, thorough disclosures. That means preparing:

- a Private Placement Memorandum (PPM), which outlines the material risks of the investment; and
- subscription agreements and investor questionnaires, which ensure that investors meet suitability standards and formally accept the terms.

Disclosure is just the beginning, though. You also have ongoing responsibilities:

- issuing regular updates and investor reports;
- providing annual tax documents (e.g., K-1s or 1099s); and
- managing investor relations and inquiries.

Once you bring in outside capital, investor relations becomes part of your job as a fund manager.

MARKETING AND DISTRIBUTION

Raising capital isn't just about documentation—it's about how you find investors.

Some sponsors raise funds directly through their own networks or marketplace platforms. Others engage placement agents or managing broker-dealers to distribute the offering more widely. Whichever route you choose, fundraising becomes part of your operational infrastructure.

Common Launch Mistakes to Avoid

Launching a QOF isn't overly complicated, but it does require precision. Most mistakes aren't obscure technicalities. They're predictable, preventable missteps that stem from rushing, cutting corners, or misunderstanding how the rules actually work.

Having seen many QOFs formed since the program's inception, I can tell you that most errors fall into a handful of common categories.

1. COMMINGLING FUNDS

This is one of the most basic and most avoidable mistakes.

Every QOF should have its own dedicated bank account. Mixing OZ dollars with other funds makes it difficult to track capital, creates accounting headaches, and raises red flags in an audit.

Separate accounts are not optional.

2. FAILING TO SELF-CERTIFY

Surprisingly, some funds forget to file Form 8996—the single form that self-certifies your entity as a QOF.

Here's the reality: The IRS does not grant automatic approval. You must self-certify starting with your first tax return and again every year thereafter.

Miss that filing, and your fund isn't a QOF. Full stop.

3. FILING THE WRONG ENTITY

Another common mistake: having the QOZB—the operating business or project subsidiary—file Form 8996.

Remember:

- The QOF is the fund.
- The QOZB is the business or property it invests in.

Only the QOF files Form 8996. Filing under the wrong entity can throw your structure into disarray and create lasting compliance issues if not corrected promptly.[113]

4. FAILING THE 90 PERCENT ASSET TEST

The QOF's 90 percent asset test, measured twice annually, is a core compliance requirement.

Failing the test can trigger penalties—and for repeated noncompliance, much worse. Whether you're managing a captive fund or raising outside capital, you must have clear systems in place to track investments and test compliance on the required dates.

Most sponsors work with a CPA or fund administrator to manage this process. It's worth the investment.

5. SKIPPING THE TWO-TIER STRUCTURE

Technically, a QOF can hold assets directly, but in practice, most funds need the flexibility and compliance buffer provided by the two-tier structure (QOF + QOZB).

Trying to shortcut that setup often backfires. It can:

- limit your ability to meet compliance thresholds;

---

113. In the first several years of the OZ program, hundreds of QOFs were flagged for investing in other QOFs. In many of these cases, this was the result of a QOZB inadvertently filing Form 8996. This letter to the Treasury Department from OZ attorney Jay Darby highlights this issue. https://www.taxnotes.com/research/federal/other-documents/treasury-tax-correspondence/attorney-seeks-procedures-to-correct-opportunity-fund-forms/7dk3q

- create challenges when raising debt; and
- complicate your operating structure.

There are some cases when a single-tier structure may make sense. When in doubt, consult your legal counsel.

6. IGNORING SECURITIES COMPLIANCE

This one can't be overstated.

If you're raising money from outside investors, you're conducting a securities offering. That means:

- filing the proper Regulation D exemption—typically 506(b) or 506(c); and
- preparing offering documents—PPM, subscription agreements, investor questionnaires

Skipping this step isn't a minor oversight. It can expose you to personal liability, regulatory penalties, and even forced rescission of the offering.

7. GOING IT ALONE

A QOF doesn't require IRS approval, but that doesn't make it a DIY project.

Too many would-be sponsors try to launch a fund without professional support. The result: structural mistakes, tax exposure, and preventable compliance failures.

At minimum, you need a CPA familiar with Opportunity Zones and legal counsel for entity formation and structuring. Depending on the size and complexity of your fund, you may also need a fund administrator to manage compliance and capital tracking.

Most QOF mistakes are avoidable. They happen when sponsors rush, underestimate the rules, or treat formation like a checkbox.

With careful planning, the right professional team, and a clear understanding of your compliance responsibilities, these pitfalls are entirely preventable.

As we have seen, launching the fund is one project. Getting others to invest alongside you is where the real work begins.

CHAPTER TEN

HOW TO RAISE CAPITAL FOR AN OZ FUND OR DEAL

ONCE YOU HAVE LAUNCHED an investor-facing Qualified Opportunity Fund (QOF), the real work begins: raising capital.[114] This is where every good idea gets tested.

You can have the perfect deal, a bulletproof legal structure, and a pristine data room. But without capital, none of it gets built. Raising money is the bridge between vision and execution. This chapter is about showing you how to cross that bridge legally, strategically, and effectively.

Understand the OZ Hook: Investor Fit and Motivations

Before you raise a dollar, you need to understand who you're raising it from and why they care.

Opportunity Zone investing isn't for everyone. It's not a mass-market product. It's a niche strategy with a very specific target audi-

114. It is entirely possible to raise capital for an Opportunity Zone deal without forming a Qualified Opportunity Fund. In this case, an OZ deal sponsor would attempt to raise capital from, or partner with, one or more QOFs. This chapter is geared toward those who have established a QOF and want to raise capital from investors. But many of the same lessons apply at the project level for those attempting to raise capital *from* QOFs.

ence: accredited investors who have recently realized a capital gain and are looking to defer and eliminate tax liabilities.

In other words, you're not selling to people with excess cash sitting in savings; you're solving a problem for people with a capital gains tax bill looming. And that's your hook. Opportunity Zone fundraising works best when you recognize this is a pain-driven market. The pain is the capital gains tax. Your fund is the solution.

Frame the conversation that way:

- Lead with the problem: "You've got a capital gain and a tax bill."
- Follow with the fix: "Here's a compliant vehicle that can defer the tax and eliminate future tax on appreciation."

For most investors, the motivations follow a predictable hierarchy:

1. tax deferral: avoid paying capital gains tax for five years;
2. tax-free appreciation: eliminate tax on future growth after a ten-year hold;
3. portfolio diversification: add exposure to private real assets; and
4. impact investing: contribute to community revitalization (a bonus, but rarely the main driver for market rate investors).

Impact may enhance the story, but the underlying investment fundamentals and tax strategy get the check written. Ultimately, the best fundraisers don't waste time explaining OZs to cold, uninterested prospects. They target those who already understand or are open to learning.

Start with:

- past investors who have worked with you before;
- your network of CPAs, RIAs, attorneys, and wealth managers—the gatekeepers to high-net-worth clients; and
- online audiences already engaging with OZ-related content or tax planning strategies.

These are the people most likely to either have capital gains or to know someone who does.

Now, here's some good news: You don't have to manufacture urgency to close deals. The OZ incentive already includes a natural deadline: investors have 180 days from realizing a gain to roll it into a QOF.

That's your built-in motivator.

So when you speak directly to that ticking clock, confidently and clearly, you stand out. You're not pitching. You're offering a timely solution to a tax problem with a real expiration date.

Remember, when you focus your message on solving their pain point, matching the investor's timeline, and aligning with their long-term goals, you stop chasing capital and start attracting it.

That's the Opportunity Zone hook. And when you understand it, everything about fundraising becomes easier.

Build Your Infrastructure: What Needs to Be in Place Before You Raise

Before you prospect any investors, everything about your fund must already exist.

Capital raising is not the time to figure things out on the fly. Investors can sense when a sponsor isn't fully prepared, and hesitation kills deals. The most successful fund managers understand a simple truth: capital follows confidence, and confidence is built through preparation.

If you followed the steps outlined in Chapter 9, you've already laid the groundwork. Beyond those legal documents, you also need operational systems in place—your infrastructure.

This includes:

- pro forma financials;
- fund administration and accounting systems;
- a CRM to track investor interactions, leads, and follow-up; and
- investor-facing materials: a pitch deck, professional website, and branded collateral.

Every touchpoint tells a story, and that story needs to be consistent: this sponsor is organized, credible, and ready to manage capital.

When an investor reviews your offering, they're not just evaluating the deal; they're evaluating you, too. They're asking: Can I trust this sponsor to handle my money? Especially with a hold period of ten or more years, being able to trust the sponsor is essential. A strong infrastructure answers that question before it's even asked.

If your infrastructure is missing or half-formed, however, every investor conversation will feel like an uphill climb. When your documents are ready, your team is in place, and your systems are built, the conversation changes. You're no longer convincing. You're inviting.

And investors will feel like they're stepping into something that's already institutional, professional, and trustworthy.

That's when capital starts to flow.

SEC Considerations and Offering Structure

The moment you begin raising capital from anyone other than yourself, you enter the world of securities law.

It doesn't matter whether you're raising $500,000 for a single-asset deal or $50 million for a multi-asset fund, the same core principle applies: if you're taking money from investors with the expectation of profit tied to your efforts, you're offering a security.

That definition comes from the Howey Test—the legal framework the SEC uses to determine whether a transaction qualifies as a security.[115] It asks four questions.

1. Is there an investment of money?
2. In a common enterprise?
3. With an expectation of profit?
4. Derived primarily from the efforts of others?

If the answer to all four questions is "Yes," you are legally offering a security, and that means you must either register your offering

115. SEC v. W.J. Howey Co., 328 US 293 (1946).

with the SEC or file for an exemption. Raising capital from limited partners outside of securities law compliance isn't just a regulatory oversight. It can mean investor lawsuits, SEC enforcement action, and even personal criminal liability for the fund sponsor.

If you are raising capital for a QOF, you are subject to securities law. In fact, in 2019 the SEC and its state regulatory counterpart NASAA confirmed as much in a joint staff statement issued specifically for the OZ program.[116]

Nearly all OZ offerings rely on an exemption—specifically, Regulation D of the Securities Act of 1933. Reg D provides two main pathways:

RULE 506(b): THE TRADITIONAL ROUTE

- You may raise unlimited capital from accredited investors who self-certify (no verification required).
- You may include up to thirty-five non-accredited but sophisticated investors.
- No general solicitation allowed: you cannot publicly market the offering.

This means:

- No public-facing websites promoting the raise.
- No social media campaigns about the fund.
- No press releases announcing the offering.
- No broad outreach to unknown prospective investors.

If the relationship didn't exist *before* the offering, it's off-limits.

RULE 506(c): THE MODERN ROUTE

- You may raise unlimited capital from accredited investors.

---

116. "Staff Statement on Opportunity Zones: Federal and State Securities Laws Considerations," US Securities and Exchange Commission and North American Securities Administrators Association, July 15, 2019, https://www.sec.gov/2019_Opportunity-Zones_FINAL_508.pdf.

- You can publicly advertise your offering via your website, social media, email, webinars, or ads.
- Every investor must be a verified accredited investor; self-certification is not enough.

Verification usually comes via a third-party service or a CPA letter. This step must be documented and kept on file.

Choosing between 506(b) and 506(c) is one of the most important strategic decisions a fund sponsor makes.

- If you have a strong network of warm relationships, 506(b) may be simpler and less expensive.
- If you need to reach a broader audience or are entering new markets, 506(c) offers scalability, provided you're strict with investor verification.

Discuss this choice with your securities attorney. It will shape everything from your marketing strategy to your investor onboarding process.

Now, regardless of which exemption you use, you must file Form D with the SEC within fifteen days of your first investor closing.[117] This is a notice filing, not an approval, but it's mandatory.

You'll also likely need to submit Blue Sky filings at the state level in every state where you have investors.[118] Your legal team will handle this, but know that these filings are time-sensitive and not optional.

Lastly, even if your offering is exempt from registration, it's not exempt from the SEC's anti-fraud rules.

That means you must:

117. "Filing a Form D Notice," US Securities and Exchange Commission, updated January 22, 2026, https://www.sec.gov/resources-small-businesses/exempt-offerings/filing-form-d-notice

118. "Uniform Securities Acts," North American Securities Administrators Association (NASAA), https://www.nasaa.org/industry-resources/uniform-securities-acts/

- disclose all material risks and facts honestly and completely; and
- avoid omissions that could mislead or misrepresent the investment.

This is why your Private Placement Memorandum (PPM) is your first line of defense. A strong PPM shows you take your fiduciary duty seriously.

As Jim Lang, a corporate and tax attorney at Greenberg Traurig, explains, "For offered funds, disclosure of risks to investors and great flexibility for fund sponsors seems to differentiate many successful funds from struggling funds. Successful funds typically have a sound deployment and QOZB acquisition strategy well before raising the first investor dollar into the QOF."[119]

Many new sponsors view securities compliance as a box to tick or a hurdle to clear. That's a mistake.

Compliance builds trust, and trust is what gets deals done.

Once your offering is structured properly, your documents are complete, and your filings are handled professionally, you're free to focus on what really moves capital: building relationships and telling your story.

Telling Your Story: Craft an Effective Pitch

When your infrastructure is in place, the next challenge is to communicate your opportunity in a way that resonates.

First, remember that every effective capital raise begins with empathy.

The goal isn't to overwhelm investors with spreadsheets. It's to connect, intellectually and emotionally, with the problem they're trying to solve. And when you pitch an OZ investment, you're not just presenting a project. You're offering a solution to a specific, time-sensitive problem:

- the investor has realized a capital gain
- a tax bill is coming due

---

119. Lang, email.

- and the 180-day clock is already ticking

Start there. Acknowledge the challenge. Then show them how your fund exists to help solve it.

A strong OZ investment pitch follows a clear flow.

1. Start with the investor's need: Lead with the capital gains problem, the OZ deferral opportunity, and the built-in urgency of the 180-day timeline.

2. Present the opportunity: Describe your project or fund in plain English:
   - what it is;
   - where it is;
   - how it qualifies as an OZ investment; and
   - why it's compelling, both financially and from a tax strategy perspective.

3. Build trust: Introduce your team and your track record. Investors are buying more than a deal; they're buying you.

4. Demonstrate alignment: Share your fee structure, any GP/LP alignment, and your skin in the game. Transparency builds credibility.

5. Close with clarity: Tell them exactly how to move forward:
   - minimum investment;
   - anticipated close date; and
   - clear next step (e.g., schedule a call, review the PPM).

Remember, the best pitches are narrative-driven. They don't bury investors in technical detail. They help them visualize the project, feel the opportunity, and see themselves participating in something meaningful.

Yes, numbers matter. But it's the story that sells. Bestselling author and speaker Seth Godin has built much of his marketing philosophy around a simple idea: marketing isn't about the products you make, but the stories you tell about them. Your story is the bridge between logic and emotion. It transforms a static pro forma into a vision investors want to be part of.

Here's what your story should include:

- Vision and renderings: What will the project look like when it's built? Paint the picture.
- Team and track record: Why are you the right team to deliver this outcome?
- Capital raise details: How much are you raising? What's the minimum investment? When do you expect to close?
- Financial projections: Use conservative, defensible assumptions: IRR, MOIC, cash flow estimates.
- Waterfall and alignment: Clearly explain how profits are split between GP and LP.
- OZ incentive primer: Briefly recap the tax benefits. Don't assume your audience is fully up to speed.
- Call to action: What's the next step? Book a call? Review documents?

As you pitch, make the investor the hero. You're not asking for a favor. You're helping the investor solve a problem and unlock long-term, tax-free growth. They're not joining your journey. You're guiding them through theirs.

Investors don't want hype. They want clarity, conviction, and a reason to trust you. When you can clearly articulate why your project matters, why it fits their needs, and why you're the one to execute it, the close becomes a natural step, not a hard sell.

Compliance and Storytelling: Dos and Don'ts

Marketing an Opportunity Zone offering is a tightrope act. Done well, it builds trust and attracts capital. Done poorly, it invites regulatory trouble. The SEC doesn't care how well-intentioned you are—if you break the rules, you're still on the hook.

With those legal guardrails in place, here's how to market effectively and compliantly.

DOs

- Operate transparently. Make sure your website, pitch deck, and legal documents are aligned. Your public messaging must reflect exactly what's in your PPM.
- Keep content factual. Share what's verifiable: project location, asset type, QOF or QOZB qualification, your team's experience, and your target raise amount. Let the facts do the heavy lifting.
- Use compliant platforms. Stick to industry channels designed for 506(c) offerings. Places like OpportunityZones.com's Marketplace and OZ Pitch Day understand the rules and help you stay within them.
- Document everything. Archive your outreach—emails, ads, webinars, social media. If you're ever audited, you'll need proof of what you said and when.
- Lead with education. Position your marketing as thought leadership. Webinars, articles, and podcasts that explain OZ rules and strategies build trust better than direct pitches.

DON'Ts

- Don't promise returns. Avoid terms like "guaranteed," "safe," or "12 percent yield." These phrases are red flags. Even implying a fixed return can land you in hot water.
- Don't cherry-pick or exaggerate. You can highlight past performance, but it must come with context and proper disclaimers. Don't make it sound like a sure thing.
- Don't mix OZ and non-OZ messaging. If you run multiple funds or businesses, keep the marketing distinct. Blending OZ and non-OZ messaging can mislead investors about what qualifies for tax advantages.

- Don't overcomplicate. Hype erodes trust. Clear, simple messaging wins.

The purpose of marketing isn't to convince everyone; it's to attract the right investors by clearly communicating what you offer. Clarity builds credibility; complexity undermines it.

When your offering is properly structured, your disclosures are accurate, and your message is honest, you can market with confidence and within the law.

Generate Leads: Building Your Investor List and Relationships

Raising capital isn't just about telling a compelling story, though. It's about having people who are ready to listen.

In private offerings, relationships are the real currency. The best fundraisers know this isn't a one-time event but rather a process—a long game. You build credibility over time so that when the right deal appears, investors already know who you are, trust what you do, and want to be part of it.

START WITH YOUR INNER CIRCLE.

These are the people who already know your work: business partners, past investors, professional peers, and long-time clients. They're your warmest audience, and often your most valuable. Many new OZ sponsors raise their first million or two from this group alone.

These early investors aren't just capital. They're validation. They become your social proof—the signal that others will watch when deciding whether to write a check.

FROM THERE, REACH OUTWARD.

Think about your extended network: CPAs, wealth advisors, attorneys, and financial planners. These are what I call centers of influence. They may not invest themselves, but they advise the people who can. One relationship with a trusted advisor can lead to dozens of investor conversations if you've taken the time to educate them and build trust.

When you're raising under Rule 506(c), you can go broader still. Public marketing is allowed, and digital channels become part of your toolkit: LinkedIn, YouTube, webinars, email newsletters, and paid platforms.

Still, even in a public raise, the most meaningful conversions still come from familiarity and trust. A click or a webinar view is only a starting point. What matters is what comes next: how you educate, how you follow up, and how you personalize the relationship.

BUILD YOUR INVESTOR LIST INTENTIONALLY.

Use a Customer Relationship Management (CRM) program to track every touchpoint. Record notes. Segment prospects by stage. Set reminders. Follow up. Raising capital isn't magic; it's disciplined relationship management over a long sales cycle. When you manage the fundraising process with professionalism, investors assume you'll handle their capital the same way.

DON'T JUST PITCH. TEACH.

Above all, lead with education. Share content that adds value: explain OZ rules, post updates on your investment strategy, share tax planning deadlines, or host short webinars that demystify the investment structure. When people learn from you, they start to trust you. And trust is the gateway to capital.

TRUST THE PROCESS.

When is the best time to build your investor list? *Before* you need the money.

Every conversation you have—every follow-up, every thank-you email, every handshake at a conference—is an investment. Trust compounds, just like capital does, and the work you put in today builds the momentum for future raises.

Never forget: this isn't about getting money from everyone. It's about finding the right investors for your opportunity.

You're looking for accredited investors with eligible capital gains—people who understand long-term investing and want to align purpose with profit. When you build a list around *fit*, fundraising stops being transactional. It becomes collaborative.

That's the difference between chasing capital and attracting it.

Leveraging Platforms and Communities

In the early days of Opportunity Zones, there weren't many places for sponsors and investors to meet. That's no longer true.

Today, a growing ecosystem of platforms and communities exists to bridge the gap, and if you use them strategically, they can accelerate your capital raise dramatically.

A natural starting point is OpportunityZones.com.

The marketplace was purpose-built to connect accredited investors with qualified funds and projects. Listing your OZ deal or fund isn't just about visibility; it's about credibility. Investors trust that offerings on the platform meet a certain standard. That trust gives you a head start before the first call is ever booked.

Treat your listing like a storefront. Include professional visuals, a crisp summary, and a link to your executive summary or pitch deck. A well-built page signals seriousness, which matters.

Another high-leverage channel is OZ Pitch Day.

This flagship event series from OpportunityZones.com brings together a curated selection of OZ sponsors and hundreds of accredited investors—live, all at once. Each sponsor presents its investment, followed by investor Q&A and direct follow-up opportunities. Some sponsors have raised millions in the weeks following a single presentation.

The value goes well beyond capital. OZ Pitch Day also offers real-time feedback. You'll learn which parts of your message resonate and where it still needs work.

Then there's OZ Insiders, my private mastermind community.

For experienced fund managers and OZ professionals, it's the strategy room behind the scenes. Inside, members trade insights, share templates, troubleshoot issues, and explore co-investment opportunities. Sponsors talk candidly about what's working—from investor communication and fund structure to back-office tools and pitch strategies. If you're serious about raising capital in the OZ space, this is where your peers are sharpening their edge.

Don't stop there, though.

Look beyond OZ-specific circles. Syndication networks, family office summits, and private wealth conferences are often filled with people who already understand the structure of private investments. They may not be OZ specialists, but with the right education, they could become ideal investors.

The key is presence. Don't just show up; show up with something to say. Join panels. Speak at events. Write articles. Ask questions. Share insights. Participation leads to recognition, and recognition leads to trust.

Trust is the ultimate lead magnet.

When you leverage the right platforms and communities, you're not just promoting a deal; you're becoming part of an ecosystem. You enter the conversation investors are already having. Then, when the time comes to write checks, you're not a stranger.

You're the voice they already trust.

Raising for a Deal vs. Raising for a Fund

Not all capital raises are created equal.

The way you tell your story, and who that story resonates with, depends entirely on what you're raising money for. A single-asset deal and a multi-asset fund may both qualify as OZ investments, but they require very different approaches to communication, structure, and investor engagement.

When you're raising for a specific deal, you've got something powerful on your side: tangibility.

Investors can visualize it. You can point to a parcel on the map, share photos or renderings, discuss the construction timeline, or walk them through lease-up projections. The project is real. Concrete. Defined.

That clarity makes it easier to say yes.

Deal raises typically have shorter timelines and smaller targets, often a few million dollars to fill out a capital stack. Because the pitch is narrow, your conversations can be too. You're not selling a multi-asset investment thesis. You're describing a building. The message is simple: "Here's what we're building. Here's where. Here's how it qualifies. And here's how the numbers work."

If the project pencils and your team has credibility, investors can move quickly. But there's a trade-off: concentration risk.

With a single project, everything rides on one outcome. If it performs, great. If it underperforms or faces unexpected delays or costs, every investor feels it. That's why many investors, especially those deploying larger amounts, prefer the risk mitigation that comes with diversification.

That's where the multi-asset fund comes in, because it is broader in scope and more institutional by design. Instead of pitching one property, you're presenting a strategy, a thesis. You might be developing a portfolio of multifamily projects. Or you may be blending real estate with operating businesses. Either way, investors aren't underwriting a building; they're underwriting *you* and your strategy.

They're betting on your ability to find deals, execute them, and manage the portfolio over time.

That shift—from project-level conviction to platform-level trust—requires a different type of pitch. You're not just answering "What is it?" You're answering bigger questions: Why these markets? Why this team? How do you underwrite risk? What's your sourcing pipeline?

And because the trust gap is larger, the sales cycle is longer.

Fundraising takes time. It requires more infrastructure, more detailed offering documents, and more robust investor communications. You'll need a reporting system, a defined investment committee process, and a higher level of compliance oversight.

But the payoff is scale.

A well-structured fund lets you raise once and deploy across multiple deals. That means fewer bottlenecks, faster closings, and greater flexibility to pursue opportunities as they arise, without restarting the fundraising clock each time.

The truth is, both models can work beautifully.

A single-asset raise can be ideal for a developer with a shovel-ready site and a clear OZ designation. A fund strategy, on the other hand, can attract larger investors and family offices looking for diversification, consistency, and scalability.

What matters most is clarity. Know what you're offering and communicate it clearly. Clarity builds trust, and trust raises capital.

Closing Investors and Managing Expectations

Raising capital doesn't end with a handshake, though. It ends when the wire clears.

The saying holds true: the fortune is in the follow-up. I've seen too many sponsors lose momentum after a promising first meeting, assuming that interest equals investment. It doesn't. A verbal yes is only the halfway point. Your job is to guide the investor the rest of the way, with clarity, urgency, and professionalism.

Think of your investor pipeline as a relationship funnel. Each stage requires attention.

After every conversation, follow up promptly. Summarize the discussion. Answer any remaining questions. Make the next step obvious. If they asked for the PPM, send it that same day. If they said they need to speak with their CPA, check in a few days later. Timely communication builds confidence and moves people forward.

When it's time to close, make it frictionless.

Have subscription documents, wiring instructions, and onboarding materials ready to go. Confirm accreditation. Walk them through the steps and make it easy to say yes. The longer you wait, or the harder the process feels, the colder the commitment gets.

But don't stop communicating once the wire hits. Send a welcome email or onboarding packet. Confirm the investment. Explain the next steps. Share contact details. Let them know what to expect: quarterly updates, K-1 timelines, reporting frequency, and upcoming milestones.

This is where expectation management begins. Be honest about the nature of OZ investing. These are long-term, illiquid investments.

Projects may take years to stabilize. There can be delays, unexpected costs, or shifts in timing. The tax advantages are real, but they don't eliminate execution risk.

Also, set the tone early. The best fund managers treat investors as partners, not customers. That mindset builds trust. And when challenges inevitably arise, trust is the difference between a panicked phone call and a patient conversation.

Closing is not a one-time event. It's a discipline.

Every investor you onboard becomes part of your story. Their experience will shape whether they reinvest, refer others, or advocate on your behalf. Deliver clarity, transparency, and follow-through, and they'll do more than commit capital.

They'll compound it.

Common Fundraising Mistakes to Avoid

Even great projects can stumble if the fundraising process is sloppy, inconsistent, or noncompliant. The good news? Most mistakes are avoidable.

After years of watching both seasoned professionals and first-time sponsors raise OZ capital, I've noticed the same errors appear again and again. Avoid them, and you immediately separate yourself from the crowd.

1. LAUNCHING BEFORE YOU'RE READY

Too many sponsors rush to market without the basics in place. They start pitching before the pitch deck is polished, before the strategy is fully ironed out, or before the onboarding process is buttoned up.

That's a red flag.

Investors equate preparation with professionalism. If you can't present a complete, polished package from day one, they'll assume your operations are just as disorganized, and they'll keep their capital on the sidelines.

2. OVERPROMISING RETURNS

There's a difference between confidence and exaggeration.

Smart investors can spot unrealistic projections in seconds. If your deck shows a 30 percent IRR and there's no serious discussion of risk, they'll stop reading. Overly aggressive forecasts signal inexperience, or worse, desperation.

Conservative, defensible numbers build trust. Promising the moon destroys it.

3. IGNORING SECURITIES LAW

Some sponsors assume that if their offering is small or private, the rules don't apply.

They're wrong.

Every capital raise, no matter the size, falls under securities law. You need a valid exemption, proper filings, and accurate disclosures. No shortcuts. No excuses.

Compliance isn't just a legal requirement. It's your foundation of credibility.

4. NEGLECTING FOLLOW-UP

Most investors don't commit after one conversation.

They need time. They need reminders. They need answers.

Yet many sponsors are bad at follow-up. They hold a great meeting, send one email, and then go dark. In a relationship-driven business, that's a fatal mistake.

The capital goes to sponsors who stay engaged and continue to nurture prospects over the long term.

5. TREATING INVESTORS LIKE TRANSACTIONS

Your investors aren't a one-time sale. They're long-term partners.

How you communicate after the raise—how you report updates, address setbacks, and respond to questions—determines whether they reinvest or disappear.

Treat them with respect and transparency, and they'll become your biggest advocates.

6. UNDERESTIMATING THE TIME REQUIRED

Raising capital always takes longer than you think.

Even with a great deal and a strong network, the process rarely moves fast. Relationship-building takes time. Getting commitments takes time. Closing takes time.

If you expect to raise $10 million in a month, you're likely setting yourself up for frustration. Start early. Stay consistent. And plan for a longer timeline than you think you'll need.

Most raises don't fail because of the deal. They fail because of communication breakdowns, compliance issues, or unrealistic expectations.

Do the basics right. Show up prepared. Follow through. Be professional. When you avoid these mistakes, capital doesn't just move; it compounds.

Raising capital for an OZ fund is never easy. But it's always possible when you align three core elements:

- Compliance gives investors confidence that you're operating by the book.
- Clarity ensures your message is simple, direct, and easy to understand.
- Connection transforms interest into commitment, because investors don't back documents. They back people.

CHAPTER ELEVEN

THE TEN-YEAR STRATEGY AND EXIT PLANNING

THE REAL TEST OF any Opportunity Zone (OZ) investment isn't at formation. It's at the exit.

For all the technical details and energy that go into forming a Qualified Opportunity Fund (QOF)—setting up the structure, selecting projects, raising capital—the most critical work comes later, during the next decade, when it's time to manage the hold. And ultimately, when it's time to unlock the full value of the tax incentive.

This chapter focuses on what happens after the capital is deployed.

It's written for fund managers and sponsors tasked with stewarding investor dollars through a decade-long journey. But it's just as relevant to investors who need to understand when and how their gains will be realized.

How OZ Exits Are Handled

Perhaps the most flexible part of the OZ structure is how exits are handled.

Investors can exit in multiple ways—by selling their QOF interest, by the QOF selling its assets, or even by liquidating at the QOZB level. All paths qualify for the tax exemption, as long as the ten-year requirement is met.

Under OZ 2.0, the window for tax-free sales is even more generous: investors can exit tax-free up to thirty years after their original investment date.

The ten-year clock starts at the investor level. That means each investor's timeline is personal. In a fund that raises capital over the course of several months or years, some may reach their ten-year mark at different points in time.

The mosaic of investor timelines adds complexity. Fund managers must coordinate exits carefully to maintain fairness, compliance, and flexibility. Ideally, a fund wouldn't execute an exit until the last investor dollars in reached the ten-year mark. This is often addressed in the QOF's offering memorandum, but it needs to be evaluated prior to investing.

Additionally, deferred gains are now recognized after five years for OZ 2.0 investments made after 2026. This rolling five-year window gives sponsors and investors more breathing room to plan tax payments and liquidity strategies along the way.

But beyond technical benefits, the ten-year hold aligns with the nature of value creation.

Real estate projects don't mature overnight. Operating businesses don't scale in a year. It takes time to stabilize assets, pay down debt, grow cash flow, and build enterprise value.

By year ten, most projects have hit their stride. That's when compounding works its magic. That's when tax advantages and real economic gains intersect.

Tax-Free Exit Mechanics

Once the ten-year mark is reached, the OZ incentive delivers its biggest payoff: tax-free gains.

But that benefit isn't automatic. It depends on executing the exit properly and avoiding missteps that could trigger premature taxation.

The IRS defines a range of "inclusion events" that can terminate the tax benefit on all or a portion of the deferred gains prior to reaching the ten-year hold target. These include:

- selling, gifting (even if to a spouse or other family member), or exchanging a QOF interest before the ten-year hold;
- liquidating the underlying investment(s) prematurely;
- taking a debt-financed distribution too early (particularly within the first two years); and
- if a manager decertifies the QOF.

Any of these actions can trigger immediate tax liability, nullifying years of careful planning. That's why understanding (and avoiding) these triggers is essential.

There is some flexibility for the QOF itself.

If a QOF sells an underlying asset, it may reinvest the proceeds into other Qualified Opportunity Zone Property within a twelve-month window, preserving its compliance with the 90 percent asset test. This rule is useful for portfolio management.

But there's a common misconception: this reinvestment does not reset the investor's ten-year clock. Nor does it automatically defer tax on any gain from the asset sale. The gain from that sale does not disappear, but it can be further deferred by investing in another QOF, which would set a new ten-year clock for that new investment.

The *only way* to achieve true tax-free treatment is for the investor to:

1. hold their interest in the QOF for at least ten years; and
2. make the appropriate election on their tax return to exclude gain upon disposition.[120]

In other words, the tax exemption is tied to the holding period of the investor's equity interests in the fund, not the timeline of capital deployment within the fund.

With these mechanics in place, the next challenge is managing

---

120. As of the writing of this book, it is unclear exactly how to make this election. Because OZ investing did not begin until 2018, the first time any QOF investor reaches the ten-year mark will be in 2028. It is expected that the IRS will clarify this ten-year disposition process ahead of tax season for tax year 2028.

the long holding period itself: balancing liquidity needs, compliance requirements, and investor expectations over time.

Managing Liquidity and Refinancing Strategies

Opportunity Zone investing rewards patience, but patience doesn't pay the bills.

While the full tax benefit kicks in after a ten-year hold, investors will inevitably face liquidity needs along the way, especially around year five, when deferred capital gains taxes come due.

Managing liquidity without compromising compliance is one of the most important balancing acts that a QOF manager must master.

The most common tool for midstream liquidity is refinancing.

Once a project is built, stabilized, and generating steady cash flow, many funds choose to refinance the property and return a portion of capital to investors. The goal isn't to exit; it's to provide enough liquidity to help investors meet their tax obligations while keeping their equity working inside the Opportunity Zone.[121]

Done correctly, this approach aligns perfectly with the spirit of the program.

But timing matters. A refinance or debt-financed distribution that occurs too early—specifically within the first two years of an investor's capital contribution—can be treated by the IRS as a "disguised sale."[122] That's a costly mistake. The safer path is to wait until after the two-year window, and ideally until the project is stabilized and producing reliable income.

Even after that threshold, refinancing must be handled with care.

In the OZ world, there are some added complexities. Until the point in time that an OZ investor has recognized gain or is subject to certain debt obligations of the fund, they have no tax basis in the

121. Providing liquidity to investors so that they may meet their tax obligation at the five-year mark is not strictly a requirement that a QOF has to provide for, but crafting some thought around this is a nice-to-have for investors.

122. Treas. Reg. § 1.707-3

QOF or QOZB. This has an impact on the taxability of distributions as well as the ability for the investor to claim losses flowing out of the QOF and QOZB. If a distribution exceeds an investor's tax basis in the fund, it can create unexpected taxable income. The risk is even higher when the underlying debt is recourse or allocated unevenly among partners. That's why every refinance should be modeled in advance, reviewed by a qualified CPA, and supported by clear investor communication.

Don't wire funds until the tax impact is understood.

Done prudently, a refinance after stabilization offers multiple benefits.

- It demonstrates project maturity.
- It reinforces investor confidence.
- It provides partial liquidity without selling the asset.
- And most importantly, it keeps the investor's QOF interest intact, preserving eligibility for the tax-free appreciation at year ten.

Beyond refinancing, funds may use other limited liquidity strategies.

Positive cash flow from operations can support small, recurring distributions. Partial asset sales after year ten can offer exit options for some investors while allowing others to stay invested. But any liquidity event, no matter how modest, must be planned carefully to avoid tripping compliance rules or triggering unintended taxes.

One rule is non-negotiable: never promise liquidity.

Market conditions may shift. Lending terms may tighten. Projects may take longer than expected to stabilize. Any liquidity event must be disclosed in advance, proportional to the fund's financial position, and supported by the fund's operating agreement.

Transparency is your best safeguard.

When handled correctly, a refinance isn't a detour from the OZ strategy. It's part of the roadmap. It meets short-term investor needs while keeping the long-term plan intact.

And that balance of discipline and flexibility is what ultimately leads to the payoff at year ten and beyond.

Coordinating with Operating Agreements and Investor Timelines

The best time to plan your exit?

Before the first dollar hits the account.

Your operating agreement isn't just a legal formality; it's the playbook. It defines how liquidity events, refinances, and final exits will occur, and who holds the authority to make those decisions. When those details are vague or missing, fund managers can find themselves stuck—caught between investor expectations and regulatory constraints.

As the ten-year timeline is the foundation of any OZ fund's strategy, the fund's operating agreement may include clarity around the hold period. That target should be explicitly stated, along with any flexibility for extensions or staggered exits. Most funds adopt a "harvest window"—usually between years ten and thirteen—giving the manager discretion to exit when market conditions are most favorable. But some funds may wish to hold for longer.

The agreement should also distinguish between types of exits.

Some investors may want to sell their QOF interest once they hit ten years. Others may prefer for the fund to sell assets at the QOF or QOZB level. The operating agreement should outline exactly how those decisions are made and whether they rest solely with the general partner, require a majority vote, or involve a hybrid process.

It should also detail how proceeds are distributed, and that includes more than final exits.

Refinancing, distributions, and redemptions must also be addressed. When can a debt-financed distribution occur? How are those proceeds allocated? What guardrails are in place to protect compliance with OZ rules? These provisions matter—not just for legal clarity, but for investor confidence and operational flexibility.

Importantly, each investor's ten-year clock starts on the date that he or she invests in the fund, not the date the fund launched or the first asset was acquired. As investors may enter the fund on different dates over the course of months or even years, this staggered timing adds complexity to exit planning. Your operating agreement should reflect that complexity and grant managers the flexibility to accommodate a mosaic of investor holding periods without disadvantaging anyone.

What Happens When Investors Achieve a Ten-Year Hold

Everything in this chapter builds toward one moment: the day your investors reach their ten-year hold and gain new options for going forward.

It's at this point that an investor achieves the full tax benefit of OZ investing—turning years of deferred capital gains into permanent, tax-free wealth. The IRS defines the technical framework, but it's your fund's planning, governance, and communication that determine how this moment unfolds.

For those who want to stay in the fund longer, they can, provided the fund doesn't divest.

Under OZ 2.0, QOF investors may continue to hold for up to thirty years after their original investment date. Any appreciation during this thirty-year period can still be excluded from capital gains tax.

But these tax-free exits require action.

Each qualifying sale triggers a personal tax election, made by the investor on his return. It's not automatic. The fund must provide accurate K-1 reporting, and accountants must ensure that OZ-qualifying assets are clearly identified.

At the fund level, this is the decision point.

Managers must weigh a range of exit strategies:

- full liquidation and wind-down;
- staggered asset sales over time;
- refinancing or recapitalizing mature assets;
- institutional exits, such as a public offering or 721 UPREIT conversion; or
- continuing to hold while buying out individual investors.

Each path has pros and cons. And each should be guided by the governance rules set in the operating agreement—ideally with clear language on who decides when to sell, how proceeds are distributed, and whether an investor vote is required.

The best exits happen at the intersection of strategy and timing, not when the calendar hits a round number.

By year eight or nine, fund managers should begin preparing investors. That means regular communication: sharing valuations, market outlooks, and potential exit paths. Investors need time to prepare for both tax reporting and capital allocation.

Clarity here builds confidence, and confidence unlocks reinvestment.

Consider an example: A QOF formed in 2026 holds three multifamily properties. By 2036, all investors have met their ten-year requirement. The manager sells one property per year from 2036 to 2038. Each sale triggers tax-free gains for eligible investors, and proceeds are distributed as deals close.

Another fund might recapitalize the portfolio, go public, or offer a GP buyout of LP interests. The structures differ, but the principle remains.

Planning turns patience into payoff. Reaching the ten-year mark isn't an endpoint. It's a pivot point when theory becomes reality, and long-term discipline begets the biggest OZ tax benefits.

CHAPTER TWELVE

COMPLIANCE AND REPORTING IN THE OZ 2.0 ERA

OZ 2.0 USHERED IN the most significant overhaul since the program's inception. What began under OZ 1.0 as a grand experiment has matured into a formalized framework—built on transparency, data, and accountability.

The Treasury Department now has expanded oversight of the program and is required to publish more detailed reports on OZ investment activity annually by aggregating QOF data from across the country.

For the first time, the American public will see hard numbers: how much capital is flowing into Opportunity Zones, where it's being deployed, and what outcomes it's producing. Congress, investors, and community stakeholders will all gain access to metrics that reveal whether the incentive is working as intended.

This marks a decisive shift.

"These reports will spur a feedback loop among stakeholders," says Michael Novogradac, managing partner at Novogradac & Company LLP. "These reports will provide information on the types of businesses and OZs receiving investment. Stakeholders and policy makers at the federal, state, and local level can review these reports and take additional regulatory and legislative steps to further spur community development in OZs."[123]

Core Compliance Tests for QOFs and QOZBs

Every Qualified Opportunity Fund (QOF) lives or dies by its compliance tests. These are the benchmarks that determine whether your fund truly qualifies as a QOF, and whether your investors keep the tax benefits they've been promised. The Treasury's framework splits these tests into two tiers: one for the fund itself, and another for the underlying operating entities that receive its capital, the Qualified Opportunity Zone Businesses (QOZBs). Together, they form the backbone of OZ compliance.

THE 90 PERCENT INVESTMENT STANDARD

At the fund level, the single most critical requirement is the 90 percent investment standard, commonly called the 90 percent asset test. Every QOF must hold at least 90 percent of its assets in Qualified Opportunity Zone Property (QOZP), which includes qualifying assets held directly by the fund, or interests or stock in a QOZB.

This test is performed twice a year, typically on June 30 and December 31 for calendar year taxpayers, using a snapshot approach.

A QOF is required to analyze its balance sheet on each test date and calculate the ratio of the total value of OZ-qualified assets divided by total fund assets. The average of these two annual tests must hit or exceed 90 percent.[124]

Miss the mark, and you're looking at steep penalties. Persistent or intentional non-compliance can trigger fund decertification, a worst-case scenario that can unravel years of tax planning and force investors

---

123. Novogradac, email.

124. The exact wording: "The term 'qualified opportunity fund' means any investment vehicle which is organized as a corporation or a partnership for the purpose of investing in qualified opportunity zone property (other than another qualified opportunity fund) that holds at least 90 percent of its assets in qualified opportunity zone property, determined by the average of the percentage of qualified opportunity zone property held in the fund as measured—on the last day of the first 6-month period of the taxable year of the fund, and on the last day of the taxable year of the fund." IRC § 1400Z-2(d)(1).

to recognize gains prematurely. Results are reported on IRS Form 8996, which doubles as your fund's annual certification of QOF status.

On paper, this is a simple math test.

In practice, though, it demands precision.

Funds with multiple asset classes, staggered closings, or long construction lead times need to choreograph capital deployment carefully. Holding too much cash (or other ineligible assets) for too long, or missing a closing window, can put compliance at risk. That's why implementing a two-tier structure is preferred by most QOF managers. This is the structure in which a QOF holds interests or stock in an underlying QOZB. And the QOZB holds the underlying Qualified Opportunity Zone Business Property (QOZBP).

THE 70 PERCENT TANGIBLE PROPERTY TEST

Once capital moves from the QOF into a QOZB, the compliance burden shifts. At the QOZB level, the most important requirement is the 70 percent tangible property standard: at least 70 percent of a QOZB's tangible property must be used in a Qualified Opportunity Zone.[125] This "substantially all" standard gives the QOZB more operational leeway than the parent fund, which is one reason why almost all QOFs structure their investments through subsidiary QOZB entities, rather than holding assets directly.

The test ensures that Opportunity Zone benefits flow to actual operating businesses and development projects in designated zones, not shell entities or parking structures for capital. Like the asset test, it's simple in concept, but real-world application requires good recordkeeping and location-based asset tracking.

THE 50 PERCENT GROSS INCOME TEST

This test ensures the QOZB isn't just located in the zone but is also actively operating there. At least 50 percent of the QOZB's gross

---

125. The 70 percent tangible property requirement is found in Treas. Reg. § 1.1400Z2(d)-2(d)(4)(ii), which implements the "substantially all" standard referenced in IRC § 1400Z-2(d)(2)(D)(i)(III).

income must be derived from the active conduct of business within one or more Opportunity Zones.[126]

The IRS provides multiple safe harbors for meeting this standard, including employee hours worked, amounts paid for services, and tangible asset usage.[127] Regardless of which metric you use, the goal is the same: to prevent businesses from parking a P.O. Box in an OZ while generating revenue elsewhere.

THE 50 PERCENT GROSS INCOME TEST: THREE SAFE HARBORS

To meet the requirement that at least 50 percent of a QOZB's gross income derives from activity within an Opportunity Zone, the IRS offers three distinct safe harbors:

- Hours of Services Test: At least 50 percent of total hours worked by employees and independent contractors occur inside Opportunity Zones.
- Amounts Paid Test: At least 50 percent of total compensation paid to those workers is for services performed in Opportunity Zones.
- Tangible Property and Business Functions Test: The business's key operational functions and tangible property located in the Opportunity Zone are essential to producing at least 50 percent of its income.

If none of the above apply cleanly, a business may demonstrate through a facts-and-circumstances-based determination that half its income is OZ-sourced.

A QOZB only needs to satisfy one of these safe harbors. In practice, most businesses qualify under either the hours-of-services or tangible-property-and-functions test.

These three tests—the QOF's 90 percent investment standard, the QOZB's 70 percent tangible property test, and the QOZB's 50 percent gross income test—form the compliance core. Fail one, and

126. IRC § 1400Z-2(d)(3)(A)(ii) and IRC § 1397C(b)(2)

127. Treas. Reg. § 1.1400Z2(d)-1(d)(3)(i)

your investors are at risk. Master all three, and you build the foundation for a durable, tax-advantaged fund.

Beyond the core asset and income tests, both QOFs and QOZBs must meet additional requirements to maintain compliance. These rules and safe harbors are designed to ensure that capital is actively deployed, value is being created within Opportunity Zones, and businesses are contributing to the program's intended impact.

THE 5 PERCENT NON-QUALIFIED FINANCIAL PROPERTY LIMIT

To prevent QOZBs from functioning as passive investment vehicles, no more than 5 percent of their assets may consist of non-qualified financial property (NQFP)—things like stocks, bonds, partnership interests, derivatives, or long-term debt instruments.[128]

There are a few exceptions. Short-term debt or cash equivalents (with maturities of eighteen months or less) are permitted under the working capital safe harbor. Ordinary accounts receivable are also excluded from the NQFP count. The intent is clear: capital should be deployed into productive, tangible investments, not parked in financial instruments.

ORIGINAL USE AND SUBSTANTIAL IMPROVEMENT

In order for tangible property to qualify as QOZ Business Property (QOZBP), it must meet one of two standards:

- Original use: The property's first use begins with the QOZB once placed in service in the zone.
- Substantial improvement: For existing assets, the QOZB must double its adjusted basis (excluding land) in the property within a thirty-month period. Rural projects only require a 50 percent basis increase.

This ensures that investors aren't simply acquiring existing assets; they must contribute meaningful improvements or launch new activity in the zone to catalyze new economic activity, per policy intent.

---

128. IRC § 1400Z-2(d)(3)(A)(ii)

THE WORKING CAPITAL SAFE HARBOR

For new projects and startups, the IRS allows QOZBs to hold "reasonable amounts" of working capital for up to thirty-one months[129] without violating the tangible property or NQFP rules.[130] To qualify, the business must have:

- a written plan outlining the use of the funds;
- a reasonable schedule for deploying the capital; and
- ongoing activity consistent with the plan.

This safe harbor is widely used in early-stage development. The key to compliance is contemporaneous documentation: keeping the written plan on file, updating it as necessary, and ensuring actions align with it over time.

THE REINVESTMENT WINDOW FOR QOFs

At the fund level, capital gains from the sale or disposition of QOZB interests or QOZB property may be reinvested within twelve months without causing the fund to fail the 90 percent asset test. This reinvestment window gives fund managers flexibility to recycle capital, reposition portfolios, and respond to changing market conditions while preserving QOF status.

However, these gains—known as interim gains—are taxable even if they are reinvested within the twelve-month period. Reinvestment protects the fund's compliance with the 90 percent asset test, but it does not eliminate the tax liability. But the gain may be deferred if reinvested into another Qualified Opportunity Fund.

Taken together, these rules create both a framework and a path forward. They impose meaningful discipline, but they also offer room to operate. The funds that thrive in the OZ 2.0 era will be those that

129. Under Treas. Reg. § 1.1400Z2(d)-1(d)(3)(vi)(A), a QOZB may apply the working capital safe harbor to multiple tranches of capital, but the total combined duration of all overlapping or sequential working capital safe harbor periods cannot exceed 62 months.

130. Treas. Reg. § 1.1400Z2(d)-1(d)(3)(v)

embrace both sides: understanding the requirements deeply, and designing systems to meet them reliably.

REPORTING REQUIREMENTS

Two IRS forms form the backbone of Opportunity Zone reporting:

- Form 8996: filed annually by QOFs to certify their QOF status, report compliance with the 90 percent investment standard,and report on economic impact across different census tract IDs.
- Form 8997: filed annually by investors to report deferrals, acquisitions, and dispositions of QOF investments.

While QOZBs themselves don't submit a dedicated form, their operational data flows upstream, which informs the Form 8996 filings by QOFs, and contributes to the Treasury's annual report.

Under OZ 2.0, these forms are no longer mere check-the-box exercises. The Treasury now requires a significantly richer and more structured data set from each fund. Required QOF disclosures include:

- fund-level details: legal name, address, taxpayer ID, and entity type (e.g., partnership or corporation);
- a full accounting of total assets and Qualified Opportunity Zone Property held;
- for each QOZB: name, address, Taxpayer Identification Number (TIN), NAICS code, and the census tract(s) in which its property is located;
- investment amounts, the value of tangible property owned or leased, residential unit counts (for real estate projects), and average monthly full-time equivalent employees (FTEs).

These expanded disclosures are not optional—they are statutory. And they transform the OZ program from a private tax election into a public reporting ecosystem. For the first time, regulators, lawmakers, and the public will have visibility into how much capital is flowing into Opportunity Zones, where it's going, and what it's producing in return.

For fund managers, this creates both an obligation and an opportunity. The obligation is to report accurately, comprehensively, and on time. The opportunity is to demonstrate, with real data, that your fund is generating real outcomes, and doing it in a way that stands up to public scrutiny.

Tracking, Documentation, and Recordkeeping

If Opportunity Zones are built on trust, then documentation is the proof of that trust.

BUILDING THE COMPLIANCE BINDER

A well-organized compliance binder is your fund's single source of truth. It houses every document that proves you've played by the rules:

- entity formation documents;
- operating agreements (for both the QOF and any QOZBs);
- IRS filings, including Form 8996;
- any working capital plans;
- lease agreements, invoices, construction logs, and improvement records; and
- contemporaneous notes supporting compliance decisions.

In practice, this doesn't have to be a physical binder; it can (and should) live in the cloud. The key is structure: organize folders by year and by entity, label documents clearly, and keep everything chronological. Back it up, and retain it well beyond the final exit.

Audits may arise years after a transaction takes place. The only effective defense is contemporaneous documentation: clear, dated, and easy to retrieve. The simplest rule in OZ compliance is also the most important:

If it isn't documented, it didn't happen.

Many QOFs outsource this entire process to a third-party fund administrator: firms that specialize in OZ reporting, compliance testing, and investor statements. These partners bring automation, consistency, and peace of mind. But even if you manage it internally, you should think like an auditor.

Can a third party trace every number on your Form 8996 back to a supporting document? If not, your records aren't complete.

TECHNOLOGY INTEGRATION

Modern compliance is a data discipline.

The most efficient QOFs don't just track requirements; they build systems that anticipate them. For smaller funds, a well-structured spreadsheet might suffice. But for funds with scale or complexity, dedicated fund administration software offers automation, accuracy, and peace of mind.

Best-in-class platforms can:

- flag upcoming test dates for the 90 percent and 70 percent asset thresholds;
- calculate ratios in real time, using synced accounting and property data;
- track basis adjustments and holding periods for each investor; and
- display dashboards with project-level cost basis, valuations, and progress metrics.

These tools don't just make life easier for the fund manager; they enhance the experience for investors.

Many platforms offer investor portals, allowing limited partners to log in, view their allocations, see basis adjustments and fair market value, and monitor compliance status. In an industry built on trust and timelines, that level of transparency is a competitive advantage.

Common Compliance Failures and How to Prevent Them

Opportunity Zone compliance isn't conceptually complex; it's procedural. Most violations come from missed deadlines, vague or missing documentation, or poor coordination between stakeholders, not bad intentions. The good news is that nearly every failure is preventable. The key is building systems that catch issues before they turn into penalties.

MISSED 90 PERCENT ASSET-TEST DATES

The most frequent and most avoidable error is missing a compliance testing date. Every QOF must measure for the 90 Percent Asset Test twice per year, typically on June 30 and December 31. If you miss a measurement, the IRS doesn't wait. Penalties begin accruing immediately and continue monthly until the problem is resolved.

Prevention strategy: Treat these dates like tax deadlines. Schedule quarterly mock tests, integrate reminders into your fund calendar, and assign accountability across your team. Your CPA or fund administrator should always review the numbers before Form 8996 is submitted.

IMPROPER USE OF THE WORKING CAPITAL SAFE HARBOR

The working capital safe harbor gives QOZBs flexibility, but only if used correctly.

The IRS requires a written plan and schedule detailing how funds will be deployed within thirty-one months. Verbal intentions or vague budgets won't hold up during an audit. And if the plan changes? The updates must also be written, dated, and preserved.

Prevention strategy: Create a formal Working Capital Safe Harbor Plan at the time of QOZB formation. Update it quarterly or when your strategy shifts. Save every version. Document how expenditures align with the stated plan. Good records are your legal defense in the event of an audit.

COMMINGLING OZ AND NON-OZ FUNDS

Mixing OZ capital with other funding sources in the same account might seem harmless, but it muddies the accounting and invites scrutiny. While technically allowed under strict conditions, commingling adds unnecessary complexity and audit risk.

Prevention strategy: OZ capital should come in through a QOF. Non-OZ capital should come in through a separate fund. And debt should come in at the QOZB level. This clear separation eliminates ambiguity about which dollars are subject to the program's rules and which are not.

FAILING TO VERIFY QOZB ELIGIBILITY

Sometimes the breakdown isn't at the fund level; it's in the underlying QOZB. If your subsidiary business doesn't meet the 70 percent tangible property test or the 50 percent gross income test, it may cause your QOF to fail the 90 percent test, putting your entire structure at risk.

Prevention strategy: Require QOZBs to maintain detailed, dated records: property leases, payroll data, employee-hour logs, compensation summaries, and any evidence that substantiates geographic operations and compliance with the 70 percent tangible property test and 50 percent gross income test.

Periodically review this documentation and archive it in your compliance binder.

LACK OF CPA REVIEW

Compliance is a moving target. Regulations evolve. Safe harbors shift. New forms appear. One of the costliest mistakes a fund can make is cutting corners on professional oversight. Skipping a CPA review may save a few thousand dollars, but it could cost far more in penalties, delays, or investor dissatisfaction.

Prevention strategy: Every QOF should engage a CPA with specialized Opportunity Zone experience to conduct at least one formal compliance review each year, ideally before submitting Form 8996.

Many fund managers also schedule quarterly consultations or mini-audits to catch issues early and course-correct before small errors become expensive problems.

POOR INVESTOR COMMUNICATION

Opportunity Zone compliance may feel like an internal function, but it directly affects investors, especially when it comes to tax filings.

Failing to communicate proactively is a fast way to erode trust. LPs don't want surprises during tax season; they want visibility in real time.

Prevention strategy: Treat your investors like partners. Issue quarterly updates that summarize project milestones, compliance testing results, upcoming deadlines, and any changes to your working capital plans. This not only reduces uncertainty but signals that your fund is managed with care and foresight.

Lessons from the Field

Compliance failures are like construction delays—avoidable with planning, but expensive when ignored. A missed testing date, a sloppy ledger, or an undocumented safe harbor plan can trigger months of remediation, expose the fund to penalties, and drain investor confidence.

But the inverse is also true. A disciplined system—calendars, checklists, quarterly mock tests, CPA reviews, and investor updates—keeps the entire operation on track. It shifts compliance from a reactive burden to a proactive rhythm.

Opportunity Zones were created to reward patient, thoughtful capital. That same mindset should guide your approach to compliance. When you build good habits early and reinforce them consistently, you won't just stay out of trouble; you'll build a fund that investors trust and regulators respect.

Building a Professional Compliance Team

Compliance is not a solo sport.

Managing a QOF over a ten-plus year horizon demands expertise across accounting, tax law, and fund administration. The most successful sponsors understand early that building a professional compliance team isn't a discretionary cost; it's a core function of the business.

A strong team protects the fund's status, shields investors from risk, and elevates your credibility with regulators and capital partners alike.

CORE ROLES ON THE COMPLIANCE TEAM

Certified Public Accountant (CPA)

Your CPA is your first line of defense. Choose one with direct OZ experience; ideally, someone fluent in both real estate and private fund accounting.

The CPA ensures your Form 8996 and asset-test results are accurate and defensible. They're also your early warning system: flagging risk areas like improperly held working capital or investor events that may trigger tax inclusion.

A good CPA doesn't just do the math; they help you stay clean.

Legal Counsel

Your attorney is your legal shield.

They structure your fund, draft the governing documents, and interpret gray areas in the code. When your fund adds new assets, launches subsidiaries, or raises capital in tranches, your attorney ensures those actions preserve eligibility under both tax and securities law. And in the event of an audit, the attorney works hand in hand with your CPA to defend the fund's positions.

Fund Administrator

Your administrator runs the back office—capital accounts, asset testing, quarterly investor updates, annual investor tax forms, and document storage. This role turns compliance into a system.

For funds with multiple assets or dozens of LPs, a third-party administrator is often indispensable. Many platforms now offer real-time dashboards that allow both managers and investors to monitor the fund.

Together, these three professionals form the backbone of a high-functioning compliance operation. Larger funds may also engage controllers, investor-relations leads, or outside auditors, but every QOF, regardless of size, needs at least this core team.

CADENCE AND COORDINATION

The most important trait of a high-performing compliance team isn't just expertise—it's rhythm. Compliance should be a standing process, not a reactive scramble. I recommend:

- quarterly check-ins between your CPA, fund administrator, and internal team to monitor capital deployment, 90 percent asset test projections, and working capital schedules;

- an annual CPA review to finalize your Form 8996 and lock in accurate reporting; and
- legal updates when any substantive change occurs, e.g., a capital raise, acquisition, or inclusion event.

Establishing this cadence keeps everyone aligned. You'll reduce surprises, improve audit readiness, and ensure your fund meets its obligations with confidence and consistency.

Understanding the Audit and Enforcement Climate

As stated earlier, the OZ program is administered by the US Department of the Treasury, primarily through the Internal Revenue Service. And while audits remain relatively rare, they are very real.

The IRS has dedicated attorneys and examiners focused exclusively on OZ compliance, especially under the enhanced transparency and reporting mandates of OZ 2.0.

The smartest approach?

Act as if you'll be audited every year. Every filing, test, plan, and update should be prepared with the expectation that it may one day be reviewed. This mindset shifts compliance from a chore to a discipline and ensures your fund is always ready to respond.

An audit-ready fund is one with nothing to hide and everything documented. It's not about fear; it's about confidence. And that confidence becomes a strategic asset.

Investor Reporting and Coordination

Transparency isn't just good practice; it's embedded in the OZ covenant between fund managers and their investors. The OZ program rewards patience and trust, and those qualities are only sustained when investors are kept informed, equipped, and confident that their filings are accurate and timely.

WHAT INVESTORS FILE

Each investor in a QOF must file IRS Form 8997 in every year they hold a QOF investment. This form reports three things:

- the initial deferral of gain;
- any acquisitions or transfers of QOF investments; and
- any dispositions or inclusion events.

This requirement continues until all QOF interests are sold or otherwise disposed of. It's not optional, and it's not the fund's responsibility to file it. But the fund must ensure that investors have everything they need to do so correctly.

WHAT FUNDS PROVIDE

For investors to complete Form 8997, the QOF must provide accurate tax documentation. The type of fund entity determines the format:

- funds taxed as partnerships issue a Schedule K-1; and
- funds taxed as C corporations or REITs issue a Form 1099-DIV.

These statements summarize the investor's share of income, deductions, credits, and any basis adjustments or distributions during the tax year.

Alongside the formal tax documents, top-tier managers include a year-end investor letter.

This letter should:

- confirm the fund's compliance status (e.g., passed 90 percent asset tests);
- summarize major milestones (e.g., property acquisitions, lease-ups, construction starts); and
- outline the road ahead (e.g., expected refinances, exits, reinvestments, cash flow to investors).

Done well, this letter helps investors understand both their personal tax position and the fund's overall progress.

BEST PRACTICES FOR COMMUNICATION

Timing is everything.

Investors can't finalize their own returns until they receive their K-1s or 1099s, so aim to deliver all tax forms and supporting documentation by the annual due date, or earlier if possible.

Beyond the annual tax packet, great sponsors maintain touchpoints throughout the year. A quarterly update—whether by email, PDF report, or webinar—goes a long way in reinforcing professionalism and investor confidence.

Some funds host an annual investor webinar or in-person event to walk through performance, explain compliance posture, and preview strategic goals. These events create transparency and give investors a chance to ask questions and feel actively involved.

WHY COMMUNICATION MATTERS

When investors know what to expect, they stay patient. When they feel informed, they stay loyal. And when they see that your fund treats compliance with the same precision as project execution, they're more likely to reinvest or refer others.

In OZ investing, transparency builds trust. Trust builds longevity. And longevity—especially in a ten-year vehicle—is what turns a good investor relationship into a great one.

Future-Proofing Your Fund

Regulations evolve. Administrations change. Markets shift. A QOF that intends to last a decade or more must be built to adapt. Future-proofing isn't about predicting every rule change; it's about developing systems, documentation, and a mindset that can absorb them.

EXPECT ONGOING REGULATORY GUIDANCE

OZ 2.0 is not the end of the road; it's a new beginning.

The Treasury Department and IRS will continue issuing guidance, clarifications, private letter rulings, and technical updates for years to come. Fund managers should expect to adjust processes and forms accordingly. Annual public reports on OZ investment activity, required by statute, will create new benchmarks and may influence future regulatory expectations.

Staying informed isn't optional.

BUILD FOR DATA READINESS

With reporting now central to the program's legitimacy, data readiness is the new compliance edge. Your systems should be able to:

- tag census tracts for every investment;
- track job creation and full-time equivalent employees; and
- record and report NAICS codes and the number of housing units created.

This kind of real-time recordkeeping is easiest when baked into your fund's operations from day one. Partnering with fund administrators and CPAs who use purpose-built platforms makes it far easier to meet new reporting requirements without scrambling at the eleventh hour.

EMBRACE CONTINUOUS IMPROVEMENT

Good compliance isn't static. After every filing cycle or mock audit, conduct a retrospective: What worked? What created friction? What could be simplified? Document those lessons and revise your processes accordingly. As your fund matures, so should your internal governance. Continuous improvement creates compounding benefits: less stress, fewer errors, and greater efficiency with every passing year.

CULTIVATE A CULTURE OF ACCOUNTABILITY

Ultimately, compliance isn't a task; it's a culture. When everyone on your team treats compliance as part of their job, not a box to check, everything runs more smoothly. Compliance becomes proactive, not reactive. Problems are caught early. Documentation is second nature. Investors notice.

This kind of culture elevates the fund itself. It makes you more professional, more investable, and more resilient. It's what separates the fly-by-night operators from the institutions built to last.

Doing Well by Doing Right

Compliance is the final pillar of Opportunity Zone success. It's how you protect the trust you've earned—from investors, from regulators, and from the communities you serve.

OZ 2.0 raised the bar. It brought permanence and additional reporting requirements, and with it, scrutiny. But that scrutiny rewards those who operate with discipline and transparency. Done right, reporting becomes more than a burden; it becomes your brand.

A fund that can show—with real numbers—that it created jobs, delivered housing, and sparked economic growth is a fund that investors want to back. It's a fund that communities welcome. It's a fund that lives up to the spirit of the program.

The Opportunity Zone ecosystem isn't just about deferring taxes. It's about delivering impact. And in the long run, the funds that do both—profit and purpose—are the ones that will endure.

The future belongs to those who build wealth responsibly.

EPILOGUE

The Next American Century

Since 1776, America has undergone a tumultuous journey; the promise of freedom and prosperity has at times seemed to dim, but it has always been sparked again.

Every century or so, the American promise revives—sometimes through revolution, sometimes through rebellion, and sometimes through policy. To the cynics, America's best days lie in the past. The nineteenth century was the great age of industry. The twentieth century was America's so-called Golden Age, and many look back to it as an American century that is now behind us. Globalization may have taken a toll on the American promise, but the Tax Cuts and Jobs Act of 2017 (TCJA) and the One Big Beautiful Bill Act of 2025 offered an unlikely new spark.

Buried deep in the TCJA legislation was a little-known provision known as Opportunity Zones. The policy didn't make headlines at first, but it held profound potential: redirect capital gains into the parts of America most in need of renewal, and reward investors not just with tax deferral and reduction, but with full elimination of capital gains on long-term investments.

With that single policy stroke, a new mechanism for revival was born. Opportunity Zones became a national experiment in turning capitalism inward, toward our own neglected Main Streets and forgotten neighborhoods. The idea was simple, even elegant: incentivize patient capital to flow where it had long fled, and in doing so, rebuild the physical, economic, and cultural fabric of America.

It was never only about tax savings; it was about a vision for a more prosperous America at a time when so many communities across the nation were underserved.

Investors who once chased yield across oceans and asset classes began to look again at the American heartland. Rust Belt towns, rural corridors, inner-city neighborhoods—places long dismissed by institutional capital—suddenly found themselves on the map. Deals got done. Projects were born. Perhaps most importantly, the narrative began to shift: from decline to potential, from neglect to reinvention.

With the passage of OZ 2.0 in the One Big Beautiful Bill Act, the Opportunity Zone initiative has matured into permanence. This is no longer a pilot program or a political footnote; it is a core part of the twenty-first-century American economic model. The updated framework rewards not only risk-taking, but responsibility. It channels capital into housing, jobs, and innovation with a clarity and accountability we've never seen before. In a sense, it is the most American idea imaginable: individual initiative meets national renewal.

The true genius of the Opportunity Zone program lies not just in what it builds, but in what it reveals. It reveals that free markets, properly directed, can achieve what bureaucracies often cannot. It shows that investors, when aligned with the right incentives, can become agents of revitalization—not in theory, but in practice.

In this moment, one marked by economic volatility, political division, and cultural fatigue, Opportunity Zones offer a rare unifying vision. They speak to the entrepreneur and the policymaker alike. They serve the interests of both capital and community. They reframe the conversation about wealth in America from one of guilt or redistribution to one of creation and contribution.

OZs can't solve every problem in the United States. But they have the potential to succeed—improving the lives of millions of citizens and strengthening the fabric of thousands of communities.

US Senator Tim Scott, the principal architect of the Opportunity Zones policy, says, "Success will be measured not just in dollars invested but in lives changed. It will mean that neighborhoods once defined by disinvestment are defined by thriving businesses, safe housing, and access to good-paying jobs. It will mean children growing up in these communities have more choices and greater mobility than the generation before them. If Opportunity Zones help make the American Dream more attainable in places that were once left behind, then we will have achieved our mission."[131]

That is the standard.

Not capital raised. Not press releases issued. Not incentives claimed.

Lives changed. Neighborhoods restored. Opportunity expanded.

OZs are not just a tax shelter. They're a blueprint for the next American century.

And so the challenge now falls to the builders: the fund managers, the developers, the founders, and the visionaries who see more than just endless spreadsheets. This book has given you the map. Now the work begins.

Go where others won't. Build what others haven't. Create what others think is impossible.

That's how we usher in the next American era.

131. Tim Scott (US Senator), via email with the author, March 3, 2026.

APPENDICES

Appendix A
The OZ Investor Readiness Checklist

This checklist is designed to help prospective Opportunity Zone investors assess whether they are prepared—financially, strategically, and operationally—to make an informed OZ investment.

- ❑ Do I understand how an Opportunity Zone investment can fit into my broader investment portfolio and grow my wealth?
- ❑ Do I currently have, or do I expect to generate, an eligible capital gain?
- ❑ Do I understand the 180-day investment window and when it begins for my gain?
- ❑ Have I decided how I want to make an OZ investment (via my own captive QOF or via a professionally managed QOF)?
- ❑ Which asset classes, strategies, and geographies do I want to invest in?
- ❑ Am I prepared to evaluate multiple Opportunity Zone funds and conduct proper due diligence before investing?
- ❑ Am I comfortable making a long-term, relatively illiquid investment?
- ❑ Have I discussed this potential investment with my CPA or tax advisor?
- ❑ Am I prepared to file IRS Form 8997 annually for as long as I remain invested in one or more QOFs?

Appendix B
The OZ Investment Due Diligence Questionnaire

This due diligence questionnaire is intended to help investors evaluate Opportunity Zone investments systematically and ask the right questions before committing capital.

- What is the minimum investment amount?
- When is the fund's anticipated close date?
- Is this a single-asset or multi-asset fund?
- Is this a blind pool fund, or is there an identified pipeline of projects?
- What is the asset class and geographic diversification/ concentration?
- Is the project fully entitled and ready to build?
- What is the track record of the operators?
- How much capital is committed so far?
- Have the GPs committed any capital?
- What tax forms can I expect (and when)?
- What are the projected returns (net of fees)?
- When will the fund begin to make distributions?
- What are the fees?

- What is the distribution waterfall, including the preferred return hurdle, sponsor promote percentage, and whether there is a GP catch-up provision?
- Is there an investor portal or other method of regular communication with the investors of the fund?
- How frequently will investors receive financial statements and other updates?

Appendix C
State Conformity

Most states either have no capital gain tax or fully conform with the federal Opportunity Zone tax incentive. There are, however, a handful of states that offer only limited conformity, and some states are 100 percent nonconforming. OZ investors with nexus in states that do not fully conform may have state tax liability on federally deferred gains and/or federally excluded gains.[132]

States with no personal capital gains tax:

- Alaska
- Florida
- Nevada
- New Hampshire
- South Dakota
- Tennessee
- Texas
- Wyoming

States that fully conform with the Opportunity Zone tax incentive as defined in Section 1400Z-2 of the Internal Revenue Code:

- Arizona
- Colorado
- Connecticut
- Delaware
- District of Columbia
- Georgia
- Idaho
- Illinois
- Indiana
- Iowa
- Kansas
- Kentucky
- Louisiana
- Maine
- Maryland
- Michigan

132. These lists are accurate as of the writing of this book, but may change over time. Refer to OpportunityZones.com for updates: https://opportunityzones.com/conformity/

- Minnesota
- Missouri
- Montana
- Nebraska
- New Jersey
- New Mexico
- North Dakota
- Ohio
- Oklahoma
- Oregon
- Pennsylvania
- Rhode Island
- South Carolina
- Utah
- Vermont
- Virginia
- West Virginia
- Wisconsin

States with limited conformity:

- Alabama
- Arkansas
- Hawaii
- New York

Nonconforming states:

- California
- Massachusetts
- Mississippi
- North Carolina
- Washington

Index

Page numbers followed by *n* refer to footnotes.

Q

R

Acknowledgments

I would like to thank the many people whose support made both my career in Opportunity Zones and this book possible:

Andy Hagans, my friend and business partner of more than twenty years, and the chief editor of this book, for believing in Opportunity-Zones.com from the very beginning, for his steady strategic counsel, and for rolling up his sleeves with me to build this book from the ground up.

Leandre Larouche, whose careful edits and substantive revisions elevated this manuscript and pushed it to a much higher standard.

Ella Ritchie and the Stellar Communications Houston team, whose editorial precision and behind-the-scenes leadership across layout, design, marketing, and sales transformed my manuscript into the book you now hold in your hands.

The Opportunity Zone accountants and attorneys who generously lent their expertise to review the technical content of this book, especially Blake Christian, Andrew Doup, and Brett Siglin, whose insights strengthened its clarity and precision.

The Opportunity Zone policymakers on Capitol Hill who thoughtfully contributed to this book, including Sen. Tim Scott, Rep. Jason Smith, and Rep. Mike Kelly, for their continued commitment to expanding economic opportunity in distressed communities.

The remarkable staff in Sen. Tim Scott's office, and in particular Shay Hawkins, for his steadfast commitment to the Opportunity Zones policy and invaluable support over the years.

The many Opportunity Zone leaders and policy advocates in Washington who have worked tirelessly to advance the policy and who have generously supported OpportunityZones.com along the way, especially Emily Lavery and Catherine Lyons.

The Opportunity Zone professionals who contributed their time, experience, and thoughtful perspective to this book, including Michael Novogradac, Barrett Linburg, Ashley Tison, Jill Homan, Jonathan Tower, and Jim Lang, whose leadership has helped shape the industry.

Gerry Reihsen, one of my earliest supporters in the Opportunity Zone industry, for generously opening doors and helping me build my network in those formative early days.

Longtime OZ Insiders standouts Frances Kern Mennone and Coni Rathbone, whose leadership, insight, and steady engagement have helped shape the community into what it is today.

The dozens of Opportunity Zone project sponsors and fund managers who have supported OZ Pitch Day over the years, especially Erik Hayden, Russ Colvin, Chris Loeffler, Michael Episcope, Louis Rogers, Matthew Iak, Jeff Feinstein, and Greg Genovese, for their willingness to step forward, share their vision, and present their projects to our national audience of investors.

Angela Hwang, John Sciarretti, Jason Watkins, and Brad Molotsky, for their professionalism, perspective, and consistent encouragement throughout my work in the Opportunity Zone industry.

My dad, Jim Atkinson, for always encouraging my entrepreneurial spirit, my mom, Mary Atkinson, for being the undisputed number one fan of *The Opportunity Zones Podcast*, and my brother, Chuck Atkinson, for being an all-around cool guy.

My biggest thanks goes to my wife, Natalie Atkinson, and to my three incredible children, Julia, James, and Kate, to whom this book is dedicated. Thank you for all of your love and support, and being the number one source of joy in my life.

About the Author

Jimmy Atkinson is the founder and CEO of OpportunityZones.com, the world's leading authority on Opportunity Zone investing since 2018. From the earliest days of the program, Jimmy has been closely involved in its evolution, helping thousands of investors, developers, and professionals understand the policy, mechanics, and real-world execution of Opportunity Zone investments.

He founded the platform in 2018 as OpportunityDb to cover the emerging Opportunity Zones industry and its potential to drive economic growth in underserved communities. In 2024, the platform rebranded as OpportunityZones.com and has since become the central hub for trusted news, analysis, education, and industry connection.

Jimmy holds a bachelor's degree from the University of Notre Dame and resides in Fort Worth, Texas with his wife and three children. Through OpportunityZones.com, he continues to educate, connect, and empower the global Opportunity Zone community.

You can connect with him one-on-one through OZ Insiders. Learn more: https://ozinsiders.com/

OPPORTUNITY ZONES.COM

About OpportunityZones.com

OpportunityZones.com is the world's leading authority on Opportunity Zone investing, trusted by investors, fund managers, developers, and policymakers nationwide.

Founded in 2018 by industry expert Jimmy Atkinson, the platform was created to bring clarity, credibility, and practical guidance to one of the most important economic development initiatives in modern history. Since its launch, OpportunityZones.com has become the central hub for reliable information and real-world insight into the Opportunity Zone program.

How to Use OpportunityZones.com

OpportunityZones.com is designed to support investors and professionals at every stage of their Opportunity Zone journey. Whether you are exploring your first OZ investment or managing an established portfolio, the platform offers several ways to engage:

1. SUBSCRIBE TO OPPORTUNITYZONES.COM

Join more than 20,000 investors, professionals, and community leaders who receive the OpportunityZones.com newsletter. Subscribers get timely market updates, regulatory insights, and access to every new episode of *The Opportunity Zones Podcast*, the world's most popular show dedicated to Opportunity Zones. Best part: it's completely free.

Subscribe for free at **OpportunityZones.com/subscribe**.

2. ACCESS LIVE DEAL FLOW THROUGH OZ PITCH DAY

OZ Pitch Day is the industry's premier deal-flow event, connecting investors directly with sponsors and Opportunity Zone projects from across the country. With more than 15,000 attendees to date, OZ Pitch Day is the most accessible way to explore active OZ opportunities.

Learn more and register for free at **OZPitchDay.com**.

3. BUILD YOUR NETWORK THROUGH OZ INSIDERS

OZ Insiders is Jimmy Atkinson's private Opportunity Zone mastermind community designed to help members gain knowledge, build trusted relationships, and get the edge for OZ 2.0 success. Whether you are an experienced OZ professional or just beginning your journey, the community provides proven pathways to connect with the right network and move forward with confidence.

Members receive access to live Masterclasses, monthly group coaching, invitations to private networking dinners, and a whole lot more.

Learn more at **OZInsiders.com**.